ommer's®

24 GREAT walks in SAN FRANCISCO

Wiley Publishing, Inc.

Author: Eileen Keremitsis
Series Editor: Donna Wood
Art Editor: Alison Fenton
Editors: Helen Ridge and Sharon Amos
Picture Researcher: Alice Earle
Cartography provided by the Mapping Services Department of AA Publishing
Image retouching and internal repro: Sarah Montgomery
Production: Stephanie Allen

Edited, designed and produced by AA Publishing.

Published by AA Publishing.

Published in the United States by
Wiley Publishing, Inc.
111 River Street, Hoboken, NJ 07030

Find us online at Frommers.com

Frommer's is a registered trademark of Arthur Frommer. Used under license.
Map data supplied by Global Mapping, Brackley, UK.

ISBN 978-0-4704-5369-8
A03625

A CIP catalogue record for this book is available from the British Library.

Colour reproduction by Keene Group, Andover
Printed in China by Leo Paper Group

OPPOSITE: MUSEUM OF MODERN ART AND YERBA BUENA GARDENS

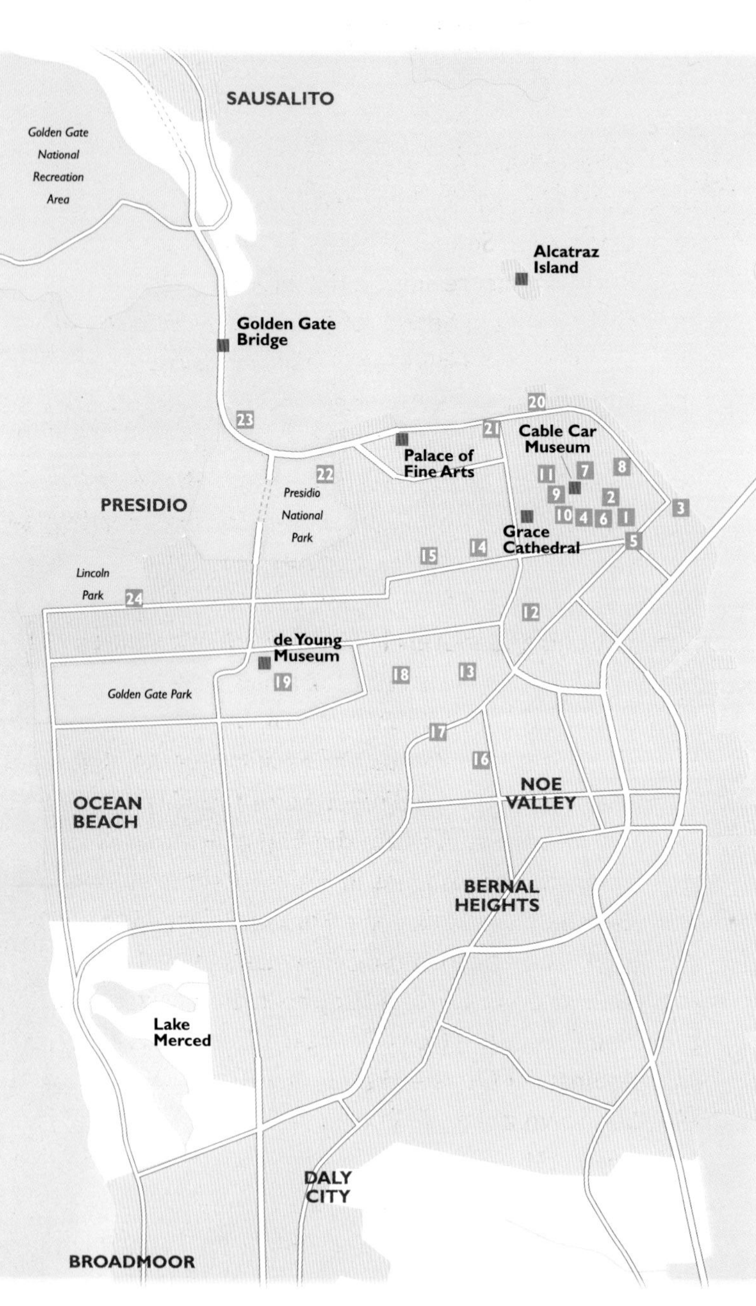
SAUSALITO
Golden Gate National Recreation Area
Alcatraz Island
Golden Gate Bridge
20
23
21
Cable Car Museum
Palace of Fine Arts
8
22
11
7
PRESIDIO
Presidio National Park
9
2
3
10
4
6
1
Grace Cathedral
5
15
14
Lincoln Park
24
12
de Young Museum
18
13
19
Golden Gate Park
17
16
NOE VALLEY
OCEAN BEACH
BERNAL HEIGHTS
Lake Merced
DALY CITY
BROADMOOR

CONTENTS

Introduction

"San Francisco is a mad city, inhabited for the most part by perfectly insane people." So said Rudyard Kipling (1865-1936) when he visited in 1889. To this day, San Franciscans take pride in their tolerance for the off-beat and edgy. The walks in this book introduce you to important figures from history, but also to the quirky side of life, taking you to tucked-away places that most people don't even know exist. You will visit well-known city highlights like Chinatown and the Golden Gate Bridge, and then venture into pocket-size gardens and meet some true eccentrics.

Some walks are short and can easily be combined; others take the better part of a day. If your stay here is brief, the first walks to try are: Eccentrics of the Financial District (Walk 1), Chinatown – a City within the City (Walk 6), The Famous Houses of Postcard Row (Walk 13), Golden Gate Park – the Park that Pride Built (Walk 19), Against All Odds – the Golden Gate Bridge (Walk 23), and Sundown at Land's End (Walk 24).

Compared to most cities, San Francisco is young. The few Ohlone Indians living here originally left no written record or permanent buildings. The first non-natives were a few missionaries and soldiers from Mexico who arrived in 1776, establishing Mission Dolores (Walk 16) and the Presidio (Walk 22). By the 1840s, a few hundred newcomers had established a small settlement at the edge of the bay. In 1848, gold was discovered inland and, in a flash, ships filled the port and the population soared to 50,000 (Walks 2 and 3). The gold rush didn't last long, but it put San Francisco on the map as the largest US city on the Pacific Coast, a position held until 18 April 1906. Debate still rages over which was more destructive, the earthquake that morning or the fire that ensued over the next three days. As many as 250,000 were left homeless but we don't know for sure how many people were killed (somewhere between 400 and 4,000). San Francisco rose from the ashes like the proverbial phoenix on the city seal. Yet she was never again the largest or most powerful western city – which is probably one reason she is so charming.

San Francisco is a small and wonderfully walkable city – and also

a city of hills. For the most part, the streets ignore the hills. North of Market Street, they cut east-west or north-south; south of Market, named streets run parallel to Market, and numbered streets hit at a right angle, which makes for some steep climbs up some seemingly innocuous streets.

Never fear! Public transport is good in San Francisco. The city's public transport network, called the Muni system, runs diesel and electric buses, historic and modern street cars, and cable cars too – all to help you get around easily. With Muni's transit packages and "passports" for visitors (available at the information centre at the Powell Street Muni/BART station), you can hop on and off as you please, without having to search for exact change each time you board. For specific route information, call 511, or visit www.511.org. To learn about cable cars that conquer the hills and historic street cars, take Walk 9.

One more practical note: Mark Twain (1835-1910) is famously quoted as remarking that "the coldest winter I ever spent was a summer in San Francisco". This is sunny California, but locals often joke that they experience at least two or three seasons every day. As you walk from area to area, you're likely to encounter even more microclimates. So, dress like a San Franciscan – wear layers!

A final word of warning, quoting Kipling again: "San Francisco has only one drawback. 'Tis hard to leave."

WHERE TO EAT

$	=	Inexpensive
$$	=	Moderate
$$$	=	Expensive

ABOVE: GOLDEN GATE BRIDGE AT SUNSET

WALK 1

Eccentrics of the Financial District

Today's bankers, brokers and attorneys are not generally considered a particularly outrageous crew. This walk proves it hasn't always been so.

San Francisco's Financial District was once full of eccentrics, and vestiges of their exploits can still be traced on this walk past some of the city's most prestigious sites. Learn about the bankrupt rice merchant who reinvented himself as emperor and issued his own banknotes (which restaurants accepted). Discover the multimillionaire real-estate tycoon who dressed in rags, begged bones from butchers, built a lavish hotel and left huge sums to establish a great astronomical observatory and some free public baths. Become acquainted with the vegetable merchant who founded what would become the Bank of America. When the great fire of 1906 superheated all the other banks' vaults and left them unopenable, his assets were ready to loan – he'd whisked them to safety in a vegetable cart and hid them behind his chimney. Who would have thought that high finance would be populated with characters like these? This walk is best done on weekdays, when the financial district is particularly lively.

1 Leave Montgomery Muni/BART station by the Montgomery St exit.

Look across Market Street to the massive and elegant Palace Hotel, the anchor that pulled the financial district south to Market Street. The partners who financed the original Palace in the 1870s were William Ralston, who died under mysterious circumstances after his investments turned sour, and William Sharon, a finicky, cold man whose tumultuous affair with a woman less than half his age led to a scandalous court battle over adultery and alimony.

2 Turn to your left up Post Street to the Mechanics' Institute, 57 Post.

When the gold rush ebbed, as many as 50,000 young men drifted back to San Francisco. Mechanics' Institute was established to channel youthful energy into productive pursuits. Now it is an excellent chess club and library. The bas relief in the lobby is of founder James Lick (1796-1876), the wealthiest man in California when he died. After his sweetheart's father refused to let them marry, he left his home in Pennsylvania, learned fine carpentry and piano-making, and amassed a growing fortune in New York, Argentina and Peru. When he arrived in San Francisco in 1846, he bought (and later sold) much of what is now downtown. He dressed in rags, never married, begged free bones from butchers (to burn and use as fertilizer in his San Jose orchards), and left most of his fortune for the creation of an

WHERE TO EAT

1 CROCKER GALLERIA,
50 Post Street at Montgomery;
Tel: 1-415-393-1505.
Restaurants, cafes and bakeries upstairs. Take a picnic up to the Roof Terrace or Roof Garden. $

2 NORTON'S VAULT,
500 Sacramento Street;
Tel: 1-415-291-7215.
A fun, friendly pub. $$

3 OMNI HOTEL,
500 California Street at Montgomery;
Tel: 1-415-273-3085.
Bob's Steak and Chophouse has a bar and great historic photos. $$

observatory in the hills south-east of San Francisco (Lick Observatory). He built a luxury hotel, which burned down in the fire of 1906.

3 Backtrack to the corner, cross the street. Next to the impressive Wells Fargo Bank at the corner of Montgomery is Crocker Galleria.

This mini shopping mall was previously James Lick Alley, situated behind the site of the hotel Lick built (the most elegant in town until the Palace opened). Pass through Crocker Galleria to Sutter Street (named for the man who owned the land where gold was discovered but died penniless because squatters and claim-jumpers left him nothing).

OPPOSITE: THE ROOF GARDEN ON TOP OF THE WELLS FARGO BANK

1

DISTANCE 1.3 miles (2km)

ALLOW 1.5 hours

START Montgomery St Muni/BART station (Montgomery St exit)

FINISH Montgomery St Muni/BART station

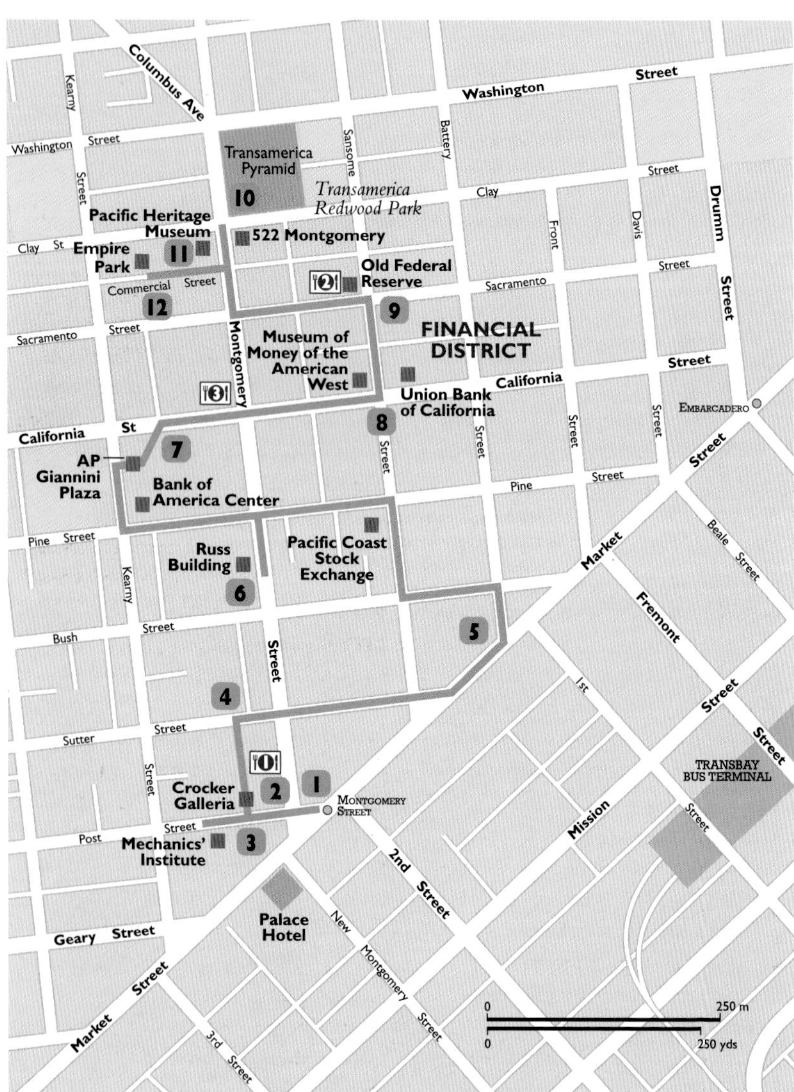

4 Turn right on Sutter to Market Street and veer left on Market. On the pavement island just before Battery Street, stop at the small monument to the inventor of the slot machine.

The first mechanical slot machine, the Liberty Bell, was invented near here by San Francisco car mechanic Charles Fey (1862-1944) in 1895. When three Liberty bells appeared in a row, the winner would receive $0.50 or ten nickels.

Not far from here, poet bandit "Black Bart" Bolton was nabbed. A stagecoach robber who terrorized the countryside in the 1870s but never fired a shot, he always left a shamefully bad poem at the scene of the robbery, signed Black Bart PO8. He was caught when the laundry mark on his handkerchief was recognized.

5 Turn up Battery Street, then left on Bush and right on Sansome (left side of the street). Peek in at the Art Deco lobby of the members-only City Club at 155 Sansome (built in 1930 as office space for the adjoining building, the former Pacific Stock Exchange). Turn left at Pine and pass in front of the old stock exchange, adorned by the two massive Ralph Stackpole (1895-1973) statues: *Earth's Fruitfulness* and *Man's Inventive Genius*, which between them represent California's combination of agriculture and industry. Since the exchange went virtual, the building has been refitted as a fitness centre. Continue walking on Pine, cross and turn left on Montgomery Street, to 235 Montgomery, the Russ Building.

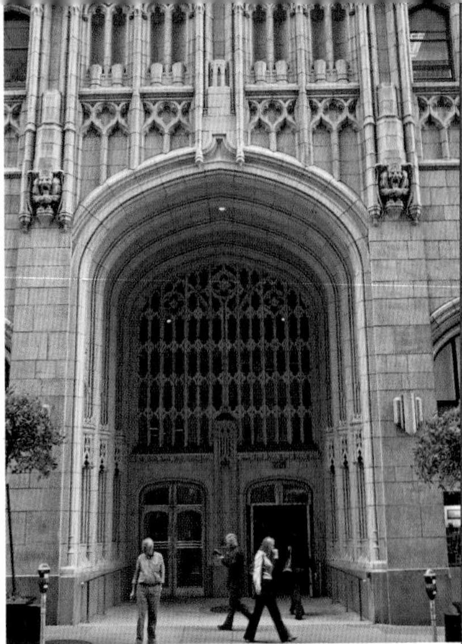

This wedding cake of a building looks like a cathedral to finance. It is named for J C Christian Russ, who came to San Francisco in 1847, used scrap lumber to build 30 rental cottages on this lot (then considered the suburbs). Rents soared during the gold-rush excitement and he turned his profits into a substantial hotel on this site (destroyed in 1906).

CITY CLUB; 155 SANSOME STREET; www.cityclubsf.com/new_art_and_arch.htm

6 Backtrack on Montgomery Street. Turn left on Pine, look up at the enormous brown Bank of America Building on your right, then turn right on Kearny, and enter the A P Giannini Plaza.

A P Giannini (1870-1949) founded the Bank of Italy, which eventually became the Bank of America. In the early years, the Bank of Italy was so small it rented space in another bank's vault. On the morning of 18 April 1906, the other bank

ABOVE: THE CATHEDRAL-LIKE EXTERIOR OF THE RUSS BUILDING

closed its vault before Bank of Italy funds could be re-secured there. As the fires approached, Giannini (a former vegetable vendor) put cash, securities and other valuables in a vegetable cart, threw some carrots on top, and in the dead of night took it all to his suburban home. After the fire was out, other banks' superheated vaults were too hot to open for weeks, but the Bank of Italy was able to start making cash loans immediately.

7 Turn right, downhill on California Street. At Sansome Street, cross and enter the Union Bank of California, 400 California. Go downstairs to the Museum of Money of the American West.

Learn about William Ralston, a prominent player in the original Bank of California, and see great displays of old coins, notes, ledgers, photographs and other artefacts at this free museum.
MUSEUM OF MONEY; Free entry

8 Exiting the bank, turn the corner left on Sansome. At Sacramento Street, look across to the Old Federal Reserve building, 400 Sansome.

The building was designed to impress. Architect George Kelham (1871-1936) used classical columns and substantial weight to create this temple to money. 400 Sansome was home to the Federal Reserve Bank from 1923 to 1983. The Fed has now moved to high-security premises on lower Market Street and this building is home to law offices. The bronze sculpture was added in 1986.

FEDERAL RESERVE BANK;
www.frbsf.org/federalreserve/visit/tours/tours.html

9 Turn left on Sacramento, then right on Montgomery Street. Visit the bank lobby at 552 Montgomery, the former Bank of Italy.

In an era of banks available only to the rich, A P Giannini was known as the little guy's banker. His desk was in the lobby so he could greet all his customers.

10 Cross Montgomery, backtrack to Commercial Street. Turn right. Stop at 608 Commercial Street, the free Pacific Heritage Museum (formerly the US Mint and Subtreasury).

The museum displays rotating art exhibits from Pacific Rim cultures, as well as a replica of an old vault with bags of gold.

11 Continue a short distance up Commercial Street to Empire Park.

Joshua Abraham "Emperor" Norton lived here in what was once the Eureka Boarding House. Norton made a fortune in the city but disappeared after he lost it on the rice market. When he returned, dressed in plumed hat, frock coat and sword, he declared himself Emperor of the US. Thousands attended his funeral in the winter of 1860.

12 Backtrack along Commercial, turn right on Montgomery and return to the Muni/BART station at Market Street.

OPPOSITE: BRONZE SCULPTURE OF HERMES AT THE OLD FEDERAL RESERVE BUILDING

ESERVE BANK OF SAN FRANCIS

WALK 2

Chocolate, Sex and Dockside Dives

A walk that explores this old Barbary Coast area of decidedly unsavoury characters, and some decidedly savoury (and sweet) food and beverages.

In the gold rush era, when the shoreline was right here and there were 50 men to every woman, this was a dangerous, bawdy district. Sailors just off the ship, or miners just in from the gold fields, could drink their fill of whiskey, lose their gold in a poker game, and maybe spend time with a lady of the evening. They could also be "shanghaied", that is, drugged, mugged and put aboard an outbound ship, only to wake up to find that they were now crewing their way to China. As the sex ratio evened out and the waterfront filled in, much of this area retained its shady element, flourishing again during Prohibition. Today, you stroll through some of San Francisco's oldest streets, past upmarket antique shops. Visit the restaurant where Alfred Hitchcock invented the Mimosa cocktail. See the birthplace of San Francisco's chocolate empire. Hear stories of true love and true lust, and about an early cross-dresser who paid for the privilege of providing maid service at the Parisian Mansion. This walk is best on a weekday.

1 Take the No. 1, 20 or 41 bus to the corner of Clay and Montgomery Street, at the base of the 853ft (260m) high Transamerica Pyramid.

On this site, the Montgomery Block offices were built, designed to withstand earthquake, fire and flood – and they did just that remarkably well for a century (1853-1959). As new office space opened elsewhere, struggling artists and literati could afford to rent studios here. The downstairs restaurant, Coppa's, was a popular hang-out (not least because artists were allowed to run a tab).

2 Walk down Clay, to the Redwood Park. If the gates are closed, continue down Clay to Sansome Street, turn left, then left again on Mark Twain Place.

During the 1860s on his visits to San Francisco, Samuel Clemens (Mark Twain, 1835-1910) met a fireman by the name of Tom Sawyer, while they were enjoying a steam bath. Twain liked the name and the man, and later made him famous. The fountain depicts Mark Twain's *Jumping Frog of Calaveras County*. Also note the plaque on the cement stairs to Bummer and Lazarus, the city's two best-known dogs, alive in the 1860s.

3 To exit the park, turn right at Mark Twain Place. At Sansome Street, turn left. Cross Washington Street, and turn left again. Turn right on Hotaling Place, stopping at the far end of the block.

The wall plaque shows San Francisco's response to moralists' claims that the calamity of 1906 was God's revenge for humankind's wicked ways:

If, as they say, God spanked the town
for being over frisky,
Why did He burn the churches down
and save Hotaling's whiskey?

The answer? Perhaps people weren't so wicked after all, or perhaps, when the firemen wanted to blow up Hotaling's to create a firebreak, someone pointed out that dynamiting a warehouse containing 5,000 barrels of whiskey might create even more problems. The buildings here and around the corner date from the gold-rush era, thanks to Hotaling's.

Look at the fire-proofing shutters on Hotaling's and other buildings – they are made of iron. When most of the city was built of wood, fires were common. (It was during the 1850s – not 1906 – that the phoenix became the official symbol of the city of San Francisco.)

4 Turn right on Jackson Street. This district is called Jackson Square but there is no "square" here. Hotaling's Whiskey had buildings at 445 and 451 Jackson, while 415-431 Jackson is the site of the original Ghirardelli Chocolate factory and warehouses.

Domenico Ghirardelli, a native of Rapallo in Italy, came to California (via Peru) and started what became a very successful chocolate business. In the 1890s, his sons moved the business to the Pioneer Woolen Mills, near Fisherman's Wharf, where Ghirardelli Square is now.

OPPOSITE: THE FROG POND AT TRANSAMERICA REDWOOD PARK

DISTANCE **1 mile (1.6km)**

ALLOW **1.5 hours**

START **The base of the Transamerica Pyramid**

FINISH **The base of the Transamerica Pyramid**

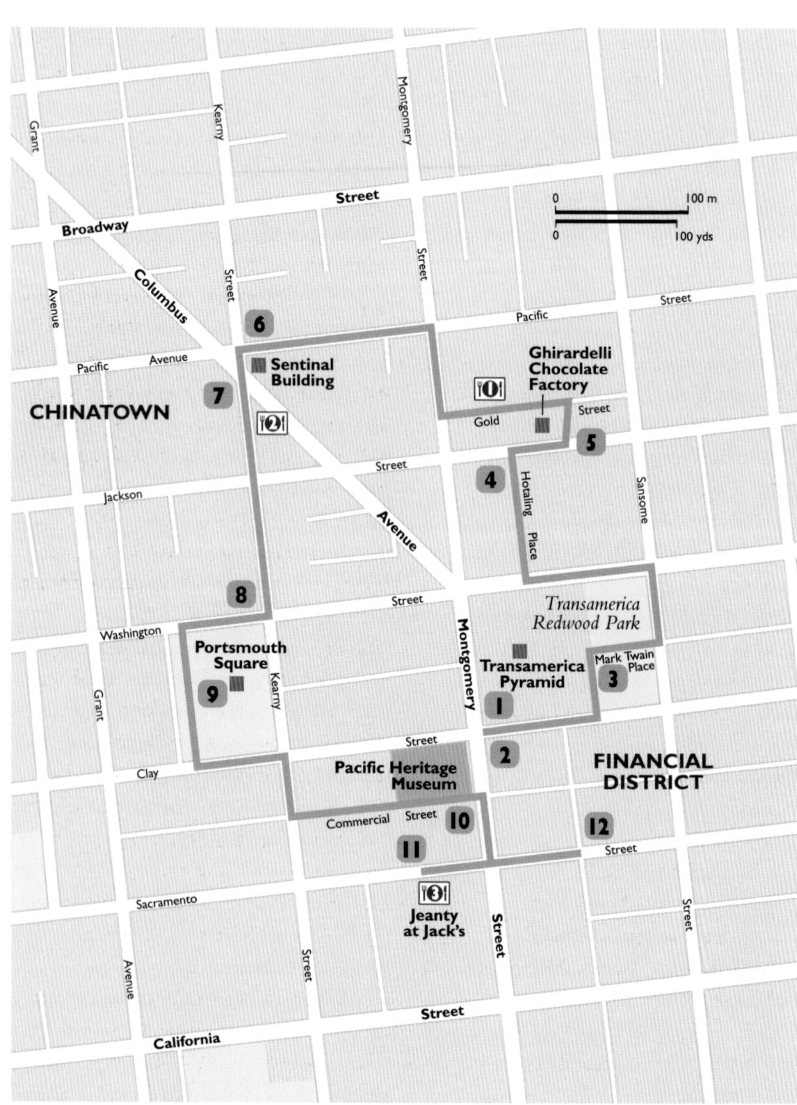

5 Cross Jackson, and walk up Balance Street, then turn left on Gold. Gold Street was named for the gold assayers working here. Balance Street was named not for the assayers' tool but for the ship *Balance*, beached a few blocks away. Turn right on Montgomery. Turn left on Pacific.

Known as Terrific Pacific Street, a 1908 police survey found 24 "resorts", cabarets and saloons in this one block alone. Before that, the brick building at the corner of Montgomery (470-492 Pacific) had a typical layout, with open space for a saloon on the ground floor, and private rooms for short trysts above.

At 535 Pacific Street, you could have seen can-can and belly dancers in its golden age. It was a distillery during Prohibition. In 1961, folk-pop group the Kingston Trio purchased and renovated it as an auditorium, and Francis Ford Coppola used it as a movie studio while working on *Apocalypse Now* and *Black Stallion*.

555 Pacific Street, the Hippodrome, was a gambling and dance hall and saloon. The current residents have kept the thematic bas relief sculptures at the entrance to the building.

6 Continue on Pacific to the corner of Columbus Avenue, and look to your left at the copper-clad flatiron Sentinel Building, 916-920 Kearny Street at Columbus.

The city's most notoriously corrupt political boss, attorney Abe Ruef, planned to open law offices here in 1906 but, first the fire, then his trial, conviction, disbarment and jail time all got in the way. Always clever, after his 1915 release from prison, he opened as "A Ruef, Ideas, Investments and Real Estate".

What is now Francis Coppola's Café Zoetrope was a Prohibition-era speakeasy.

7 Turn left on Kearny Street and pass the Sentinel Building.

Crossing Jackson Street, you pass near what was the Hotel Nymphia, a brothel-hotel owned by Twinkling Star Corporation from 1899 to 1903. They'd hoped to fill the 450 rooms with nymphomaniacs who would work for free, but even with "working girls" who required payment, Twinkling Star still made a tidy profit.

8 At Washington Street, turn right uphill and enter Portsmouth Square.

The original centre of town is now a gathering place for Chinatown residents. The historic markers don't mention that the early town's best gambling halls and saloons were located around the square. Irene McCready and Belle Cora, both well-known gold-rush era madams, had brothels within a block. Don't miss the monument with Robert Louis Stevenson's (1850-94) wistful, romantic poetry.

9 Continue across Portsmouth Square to Clay Street, turn left (downhill). Cross and turn right on Kearny Street, then left on Commercial Street.

JEANTY AT JACK'S
JEANTY
615

In the 19th century, this was the French Quarter, home to bordellos like the Parisian Mansion at 742 Commercial. Fathers brought their sons here to learn the ways of love. Also, one man, a cross-dresser, had an unusual arrangement with the madam – he arrived every morning dressed in street clothes, changed into a maid's costume, cleaned the establishment top to bottom, paid $5, changed back into street clothes, and left. For a time, odd-ball inventor Rube Goldberg (1883-1970) owned a building (that was never a brothel) at 755 Commercial.

10 Turn right on Montgomery Street, then cross and turn right on Sacramento Street to Jeanty at Jack's, 615 Sacramento.

With roots to 1864 (rebuilt after 1906), Jack's had a classic "French restaurant" set-up with two entrances. Families entered through the main door to enjoy a sumptuous meal in the ground-floor dining room. The alternate entrance, which opened on to the elevator, was reserved for clientele seeking discrete encounters. Upper floors provided private dining rooms, each with a couch or bed. You can still see the second-floor private rooms but all are now open, and the food they serve is excellent. Clark Gable, Cary Grant, Ingrid Bergman, Frank Sinatra and Ernest Hemingway are among the notables who enjoyed eating and drinking at Jack's. And they say that one morning, nursing a mean hangover, Alfred Hitchcock concocted the Mimosa here, mixing his orange juice with champagne.

WHERE TO EAT

1 BIX RESTAURANT,
56 Gold Street;
Tel: 1-415-433-6300.
A jazz club in what was once a gold assayer's office. $$$

2 CAFÉ ZOETROPE,
916 Kearny Street;
Tel: 1-415-291-1700.
Light cafe fare and also full Italian meals. $$

3 JEANTY AT JACK'S,
615 Sacramento Street;
Tel: 1-415-693-0941.
Good food, but still worth a visit to check out the upstairs rooms. $$

11 Backtrack on Sacramento to the plaque commemorating the What Cheer House, at the corner of Leidesdorff.

In counterpoint to the bawdy ways of old San Francisco, the temperance hotel What Cheer House had strict policies: no women or alcohol allowed!

The street was named for William Leidesdorff (1810-48), a businessman, ship captain, waterfront trader and smuggler. A mulatto, he came to San Francisco from New Orleans in 1841, after his true love's father shunned him for his race.

12 To return to the Transamerica Pyramid, backtrack on Sacramento Street and turn right at Montgomery.

OPPOSITE: JEANTY AT JACK'S RESTAURANT, WHERE HITCHCOCK REPUTEDLY INVENTED THE MIMOSA COCKTAIL

THE COPPER-CLAD SENTINEL BUILDING, WITH THE TRANSAMERICA PYRAMID TOWERING BEHIND

PLANT

WALK 3

Buried Treasure on the Waterfront

A stroll over what was once the bay and the waterfront, crossing a nautical graveyard, and passing many previously buried treasures.

Native Americans traditionally fished and hunted here along the shores of the bay. When gold was discovered and the world rushed in, tidal waters reached at least half a mile (0.8km) inland from where they do now. Gold-rush era ships were abandoned in port. Some sunk in the mud; some were used as offices, warehouses, stores and hotels until fires destroyed everything above the water line. Rubble from the ships was mixed with sand from nearby dunes to create buildable dry land. Luckily for us, over the past few decades whenever a foundation is dug for a downtown skyscraper, there's an archaeologist on site to note the "historical value of submerged cultural resource". The prosaic submerged cultural resources include shell mounds, jars of olives, bottles of champagne, guns, nails, porcelain, and even entire ship hulls. In a city of hills, it's no coincidence that this walk stays on the flat. You'll be walking over land flattened when it was filled in. Two hundred years ago, you would have been climbing sand dunes or walking on water or mud, but today it's nicely paved!

1 **Take the F-Market street car or any of the buses or trolleys that stop at Embarcadero. (From Embarcadero Muni station, take the Spear Street exit.) Walk along Market Street towards the Ferry Building to the corner of Steuart Street.**

While digging the tunnel to bring the underground Muni railway south to the new ballpark, construction workers – and archaeologists – were surprised to find remnants of the gold-rush era ship *Rome* buried under what is now a park here.

2 **Turn right on Steuart Street. At Mission Street, cross and enter the Rincon Center.**

This building – now holding offices, restaurants and apartments – is the proud result of "adaptive reuse", with a lobby that still looks much like it did from the time it was a post office (except now there are no queues). To get an overview of San Francisco history, don't miss the murals. Their "leftist" leaning was the source of much controversy when they were first unveiled.

Long before the post office was here, this was the site of a boarding house for sailors. Excavations have uncovered domestic items such as crockery, glass bottles, metal objects and a large amount of Chinese porcelain (indicating that there was a Chinese restaurant or laundry nearby).

3 **Continue on Mission Street, and cross Spear Street to 100 Spear.**

The giant propeller out front reflects the owner's love of things nautical. In the lobby of this office building are models of the types of ship that brought newcomers to San Francisco. (Open weekdays only.)

4 **Continue on Mission to 1st Street. Cross 1st Street and turn right. Just at Market Street on the left is a plaque marking the original shoreline.**

In the gold-rush era, what is now Market Street from here past the Ferry Building was the city's second-longest wharf. All along the route you are walking over buried treasure. Not only have you stepped over remains of the ships *Othello, Byron, Callao, Panama* and *Trescott*, but between and beyond these ships was a different kind of treasure: real estate. After the US claimed California,

OPPOSITE: MURAL AT THE RINCON CENTER; ABOVE: THE GIANT BRASS PROPELLER ON SPEAR STREET

DISTANCE 2 miles (3.2km)

ALLOW 2 hours

START AND FINISH Embarcadero Muni/BART station (Spear St exit), or Ferry Building stop on F-Market street car

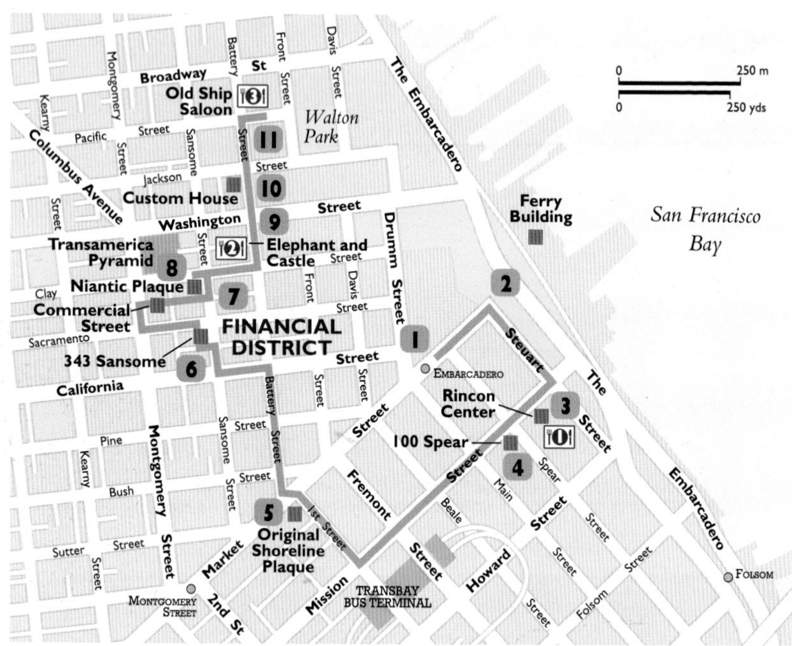

the government sold lots that didn't exist, hoping to meet two goals at once: generate money and fill in the bay. Lines of posts were planted in the mud, marking off "water lots", which were submerged at high tide but supposed to be dry at low tide – in fact, some never saw air. The government generated some income, but those who bought and sold generated much more. Lots selling for \$16 to \$50 in 1848, resold for \$40 to \$100 in 1849, and for \$8,000 to \$16,000 four years later.

5 Cross Market, and walk north on Battery Street. At California Street (site of another old wharf), turn left one block, then right on Sansome Street. Just past Halleck Street, enter 343 Sansome.

To your right in the lobby is a display of items found during the 1989 excavations under the site of this office building, presumably from a gold-rush era dockside store. For a bird's-eye view of the territory you've covered, take the elevator to the public roof garden on the 15th floor.

OPPOSITE: THE PUBLIC ROOF GARDEN ON THE 15TH FLOOR AT 343 SANSOME

WHERE TO EAT

1 FOOD COURT AT THE RINCON CENTER,
121 Spear Street;
Tel: 1-415-777-4100.
Popular lunchtime food court with an amazing indoor waterfall. $

2 ELEPHANT & CASTLE PUB,
425 Battery Street at Clay;
Tel: 1-415-268-3900.
Fun pub over the remains of the *General Harrison*. $$

3 OLD SHIP SALOON,
298 Pacific Avenue at Battery;
Tel: 1-415-788-2222.
Sandwiches and other light fare. $$

6 Returning to ground level, exit the elevator through the corridor past the kinetic sculpture of floating metal balls. Leaving the building, turn left on Sacramento Street, right on Montgomery, and right again on Commercial.

Commercial Street was the original aptly named "Long Wharf", the centre of activity during the gold-rush excitement.

7 At Sansome Street turn left, cross Clay and look for the plaque on the Clay Street side of the corner building.

This is the site of the *Niantic.* After the crew had left for the gold fields, the ship *Niantic* was sold to local entrepreneurs, who pushed and pulled and rolled it at high tide, until it was at the shoreline along the Long Wharf. They covered it with a shingle roof. The deck was partitioned into stores and offices, and doors were cut into the hull, which was turned into storage. Rentals brought in an astronomical $20,000 per month. After the great fire in May 1851, in which the *Niantic* was burned to the waterline, the site was filled in and a Niantic Hotel built above the ruins. An 1872 excavation of the site found 35 baskets of Jacquesson Fils champagne (still drinkable, they say) in the mud below. Then, in 1978, when new construction required even deeper foundations, they found another 13 bottles of champagne, along with numerous other artifacts.

8 Backtrack down Clay Street to Battery Street, where you'll find the Elephant & Castle, 425 Battery.

During the 2001 excavation here, archaeologists found the intact hull of the *General Harrison*, approximately 127ft (39m) long, 26ft (7.9m) broad and 13ft (4m) deep, with a bilge section 82ft (25m) long. The bow remains buried under a previously existing building. Spend a moment contemplating the curving lines on the path – they are designed to show the outline of the hull below.

Stop in for a pint if you like, and feel grateful that you no longer need to worry about Shanghai. This would have been a problem in the 1800s, when many a ship that arrived in port lost its crew (and often its officers) immediately to the gold rush – some ships (like the *General Harrison*) never again left port. But for those captains who wanted to return to sea, finding crew could be a challenge. A sailor's life was hard, and the opportunities on shore were great. The answer? Shanghai. Young men – experienced sailors or not – who visited the dockside dives, would be offered apparently fine beer, whiskey or cigars. Laced with opium or laudanum, the offerings knocked the boys out and the next thing they knew they were on the high seas, sailing for Shanghai or other distant ports.

9 Turn left on Battery. Just past Washington Street, pass in front of the Custom House.

The ships *Georgian* and *Louisa* lie underground here. And, just a few blocks "inland" (off Jackson Street near Sansome) is Balance Street, one of the city's shortest streets. It's in a district where gold assayers plied their trade but the street is named for a ship not an assayer's tool. When *Balance* arrived in port here, it belonged to an American. He'd captured it from the British, which he felt balanced the score, as earlier they had captured one from him. The *Balance* was beached at round about Jackson and Front, and he had the nearest unnamed street named in its honour.

The Custom House's massive size and architecture reflect the federal government's imposing presence in the days when this was the busiest west-coast port. Before income tax, the duties collected on imports and exports were a major source of revenue for the national government. (The Custom House is now closed for security reasons.)

10 Continue on Battery Street to Pacific Avenue, and the Old Ship Saloon, 298 Pacific.

The remains of the *Arkansas* are buried here. Don't miss the historic photos on the walls.

11 To return to your starting point at the Ferry Building, walk down Pacific to the park at Front Street, turn right, then left on Jackson, right on Drumm Street, left on Washington and right along the Embarcadero.

ABOVE: THE HISTORIC FERRY BUILDING AND CLOCKTOWER ON THE WATERFRONT

WALK 4

Downtown in Search of the Maltese Falcon

Walk in the footsteps of Dashiell Hammett, father of hard-boiled American detective fiction, who lived and wrote here in the 1920s.

Samuel Dashiell Hammett (1894–1961) was a less than stellar student (he left school at 14) or employee (he worked on the Baltimore & Ohio Railroad, in factories, at stockbrokers' and in casual jobs). But when he answered a mysterious newspaper ad and "found himself" employed at Pinkerton National Detective Agency, life turned around. Little routine and lots of travel, novelty and danger with Pinkerton's appealed to young Hammett, at least for a time. In a veterans' hospital for a flare-up of tuberculosis, he fell in love with nurse Josephine Dolan. It was with Josephine that Dashiell Hammett came to San Francisco, worked for the local branch of Pinkerton's, and started to write and publish detective stories. This walk concentrates on the core locales of Hammett's life in San Francisco, and those of his characters: Sam Spade, Brigid O'Shaughnessy, the Continental Op, the fat man, and their friends and adversaries. It also takes in Union Square, San Francisco's long-time retail centre, and skirts through Little Paris, the Financial District, the theatre district, and the edges of the scruffy Tenderloin.

1 Get off the Powell Street cable car at Pine Street and Powell. Walk east on Pine, then turn right (downhill) to 20 Dashiell Hammett Street (formerly Monroe Street).

While Josephine and their children still lived several blocks away (at 620 Eddy Street), Hammett took a room here, where he could concentrate on his writing – and drinking – by night, while he wrote advertising copy for Samuels Jewelers during the day.

Monroe Street was renamed for Hammett in 1988, at the same time more small streets in the city were renamed for other literati: Mark Twain, Jack London, Frank Norris, Richard Henry Dana, Isadora Duncan, Benny Bufano, Bob Kaufman, Ambrose Bierce, Jack Kerouac, Kenneth Rexroth, and William Saroyan. The street sign has changed, but notice that Monroe is still stamped into the pavement at the corner. It is said that people lost their bearings after the 1906 fires wiped out street signs, and now street names appear in the cement, where fires can't erase them.

2 Continue on Hammett Street to Bush. Turn left on Bush to Stockton, cross, and backtrack uphill a few feet to Burritt Alley.

In *The Maltese Falcon*, Sam Spade gets a late-night telephone call to come here, where "Bush Street roofed Stockton" to identify the body of his partner, Miles Archer, who was done in by Brigid O'Shaughnessy. Note the wall plaque.

WHERE TO EAT

1 JOHN'S GRILL,
63 Ellis Street;
Tel: 1-415-986-0069.
Enjoy a drink or a full meal in the ambience that Hammett enjoyed. $$

2 TUNNEL TOP BAR,
601 Bush Street near Burritt Alley;
Tel: 1-415-986-8900.
Drinks and music. $$

3 CAFÉ CLAUDE,
7 Claude Lane;
Tel: 1-415-392-3505.
A Little Paris bistro. $$

3 Return downhill on Bush to Grant Avenue, turn right and pause at the large building on your right: Home Telephone Company, 333 Grant.

In the 1920s, many telephone calls were routed through the operating exchange on the upper floors of this building. Home Telephone got its start in the city in a rather scandalous event two decades prior. After the original Bell Telephone patents expired at the turn of the century, the Midwest-based Home Telephone Company tried to break Bell's monopoly on telephone service in various markets nationwide. Hoping for a share of the lucrative San Francisco market, Home Telephone directors paid hefty bribes to notoriously corrupt San Francisco politicians, in return for a favourable vote at the franchise hearing scheduled for

OPPOSITE: MONROE STREET WAS RENAMED DASHIELL HAMMETT STREET IN 1988

DISTANCE 1.5 miles (2.5km)

ALLOW 1.5 hours

START Pine Street at Powell Street

FINISH Powell Street at Market Street

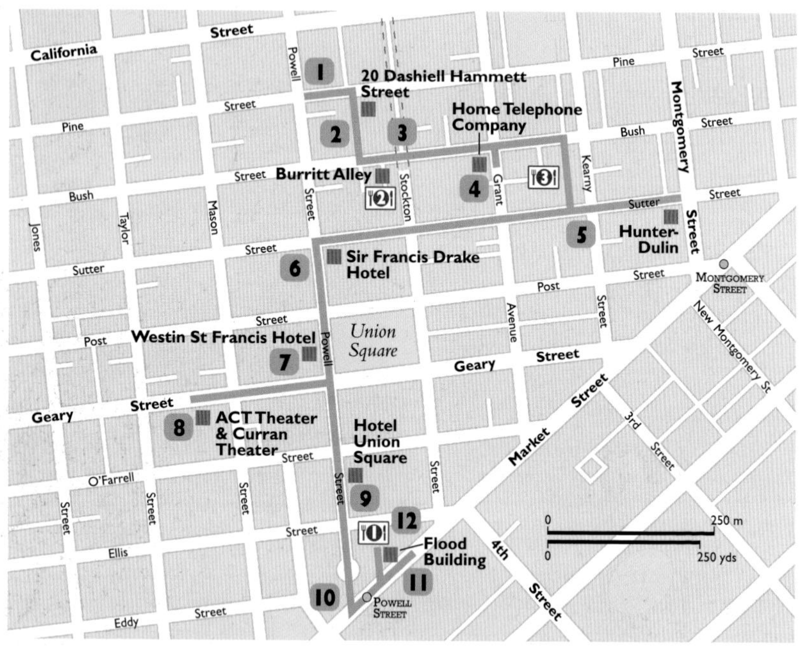

Monday 23 April 1906. As fate would have it, on Wednesday 18 April, the Great Quake started the fires that burned through the city until 21 April. With the city in shambles and maybe a quarter of a million residents now homeless, Home Telephone directors still insisted that the hearing be held as scheduled – in the saloon belonging to one of the corrupt politicians – and lo and behold, the Home Telephone Company was successful in the franchise bid! (They later merged with the Bell company.)

4 Backtrack on Grant to Bush Street and continue right, through Little Paris. Turn right on Claude Lane.

Sam Spade often eluded followers by slipping down little alleys like this. In another mystery – Alfred Hitchcock's *Vertigo* – Scottie trails Madeleine's green Jaguar down Claude Lane. As Claude Lane ends at Sutter Street, look left at the copper-roofed building across the street and a block away. This distinctive roofline belongs to the Hunter-Dulin

OPPOSITE: THE HUNTER-DULIN BUILDING WITH ITS DISTINCTIVE COPPER-CRESTED ROOFLINE

Building, 111 Sutter, where Sam Spade had offices. To get there, walk the one block on Sutter to Montgomery, and cross the street. Hammett gave Sam Spade offices here when the building was new. Spade's office was probably less elegant than either the building's distinctive exterior – with its copper-crested roofline and the terracotta façade – or the small but elegant lobby. (They say the circular depression in the lobby's marble floor is the result of decades of wear from the doorman's foot, as he pivoted to point people to the next available elevator.)

5 Turn left on Sutter to Hunter-Dulin. As you leave, backtrack along Sutter. At Powell Street, turn left (downhill). Sir Francis Drake Hotel is on the corner of Powell and Sutter.

Some say one of the contenders for the Maltese falcon, fat man Caspar Gutman, stayed here. But even if he didn't, the doorman is a San Francisco institution and well worth checking out regardless.

6 Continue down Powell to Union Square. On your right is the Westin St Francis Hotel, 335 Powell.

Miles Archer may have tailed Brigid O'Shaunessey from the St Francis lobby to Burritt Alley, where she shot him. Also, in September 1921, Hammett probably helped gather evidence here for Pinkerton's in the case of silent film star Roscoe "Fatty" Arbuckle's alleged rape and murder of actress Virginia Rappe at a weekend party, in rooms 1219 and 1221.

7 As you leave the St Francis, turn right down to the corner, and turn right again on Geary Street for just over a block to the Geary Theater (now ACT Theater), 415 Geary, where Sam Spade waited for Joel Cairo, who had tickets to attend a performance there.

Notice also the Curran Theatre next door, at 445 Geary. Peek through the windows into the lobby and see if you can spot the ghost of the ticket-taker who was shot in a bungled robbery in the 1930s – sometimes he appears in the mirror. Note that Geary is pronounced GEAR-ee.

8 Backtrack on Geary to Powell Street. Cross and turn right to the Hotel Union Square, 114 Powell.

In Hammett's day, this was the Golden West Hotel, built in 1913 for the many visitors to the 1915 Panama-Pacific International Exposition. On the eve of their 1921 wedding, Hammett booked a suite here for his bride-to-be, Josephine Dolan. Years later, after his marriage went sour, he got together with author Lillian Hellman. We don't know for sure when Lillian stayed here but her ghost has been seen lingering about room 207.

HOTEL UNION SQUARE;
114 POWELL STREET; www.hotelunionsquare.com

9 Continue walking down Powell Street to Market Street.

Walk a short way along Market Street and look back up at the flatiron building that you just passed on the left: the Flood

Building, 870 Market. Pinkerton's had offices on the third floor.
(For a history of the Flood building, see www.floodbuilding.com)

10 **Turn left in front of the Flood Building, a small distance from Samuels Jeweler's clock on the pavement in front of 856 Market Street.**

Hammett was writing stories while he worked as advertising manager and copywriter for A S Samuel's in the mid-1920s. When his tuberculosis returned, he retired from Samuel's with total disability benefits from the Veteran's Administration.

11 **Backtrack to Market to the Flood Building, pass through the lobby (check out the historic elevators that date back to 1904) or, if the building is closed, walk around it back up Powell Street to Ellis Street. As you exit the Flood Building at Ellis, enter John's Grill, 63 Ellis.**

Hard-drinking Hammett certainly drank alone but he also enjoyed the camaraderie at John's. Ask to visit the Maltese Falcon and Dashiell Hammett museum in the upstairs dining room.

JOHN'S GRILL;
63 ELLIS STREET; www.johnsgrill.com

12 **When you leave John's, turn left on Ellis, then left again almost immediately at Powell Street. In one block, you'll be at the Powell Street cable car terminus, and just upstairs from the Powell Street Muni/BART station.**

ABOVE: HAMMETT WAS A COPYWRITER FOR SAMUELS JEWELERS, WHOSE CLOCK STILL STANDS

THE ORNATE GEARY THEATER, NOW HOME TO THE AMERICAN CONSERVATORY THEATER

TRAGEDY

WALK 5

Gardens and Galleries of Market Street

A walk through the city's surprisingly verdant business district – where far-seeing city planners mixed high-rises with beautiful public spaces.

This walk takes you along crowded, noisy downtown Market Street. You'll weave in and around high-rise office buildings. You'll skirt the financial district, and an area south of Market Street that was once a less than desirable residential and manufacturing district. But never fear! There's a surprising array of pocket-sized parks, roof gardens, sunny corners and "secret" little art galleries. Cool yourself by fountains. Listen to free concerts at noontime. Picnic in a bamboo forest. The walk takes you by San Francisco's first "skyscraper", constructed in 1889 and now converted into luxury time-share hotel suites. A century later, city planners became alarmed about the "Manhattanization" of San Francisco. New codes required that downtown office buildings soften the sharp edges with some kind of public space. Some are little more than an extra-wide pavement, but others are true oases. At lunchtime, the office towers seem to drain and little parks fill with workers. This walk is best done Tuesday to Friday, when the galleries are open, the fountains are flowing and the streets are bustling.

1 As you leave Montgomery Street station (Sansome-Sutter exit), pass through the massive columns on your left at 1 Sansome Street, Citigroup Center.

The old main banking hall (originally the London Paris National Bank) is now a skylight-covered, marble-lined open space (the developers' trade-off for building a huge monolith behind). Say hello to the Star Girl, a bronze replica of the 1915 Panama-Pacific International Exposition theme statue.

2 Cross Sansome Street to the Crown-Zellerbach Building, 1 Bush Street at Market Street.

The open space at this 1959 building wasn't required by law but was included as part of the award-winning design. It is now used by office workers needing a smoke. The vibrant social scene is at street level, where bike messengers congregate.

Looking at Market Street, consider its width. When a young man chooses a profession, generally speaking the true dare-devils don't pursue map-making. Irish surveyor Jasper O'Farrell must have been unsettled by his near-lynching in the 1840s. His crime? Expanding and correcting the city map, disregarding topography and creating Market Street, a wide thoroughfare that connected the port with the city's other main population centre, the old Mission. You might want to pummel him for this, as you huff and puff up hills, but that wasn't the issue in his day. It was Market Street's 120ft (37m) width. Property owners about to lose their land to the city for Market Street saw no reason for such excessive width, and assembled a vigilante team to tar and feather O'Farrell. Luckily, he was tipped off and escaped.

3 Walk left on Market Street to Battery. Cross and return on Market to the park, just before 555 Market. Turn left through the park, the site of noon-time concerts and a fountain.

The buildings on either side were partially responsible for the fear of Manhattanization. One architectural historian calls 525 Market "an immense blockbuster without scale clues".

4 At the back of the park is Ecker Street. Continue to the pocket park at Jessie and Ecker. Who would expect

OPPOSITE: ROOF GARDENS ABOVE WELLS FARGO; ABOVE: J P MORGAN-CHASE PLAZA

DISTANCE 1.5 miles (2.5km) – some hills

ALLOW 1 hour (longer if you visit the museums)

START Montgomery St Muni/BART station (Sansome-Sutter exit)

FINISH Powell St Muni/BART station

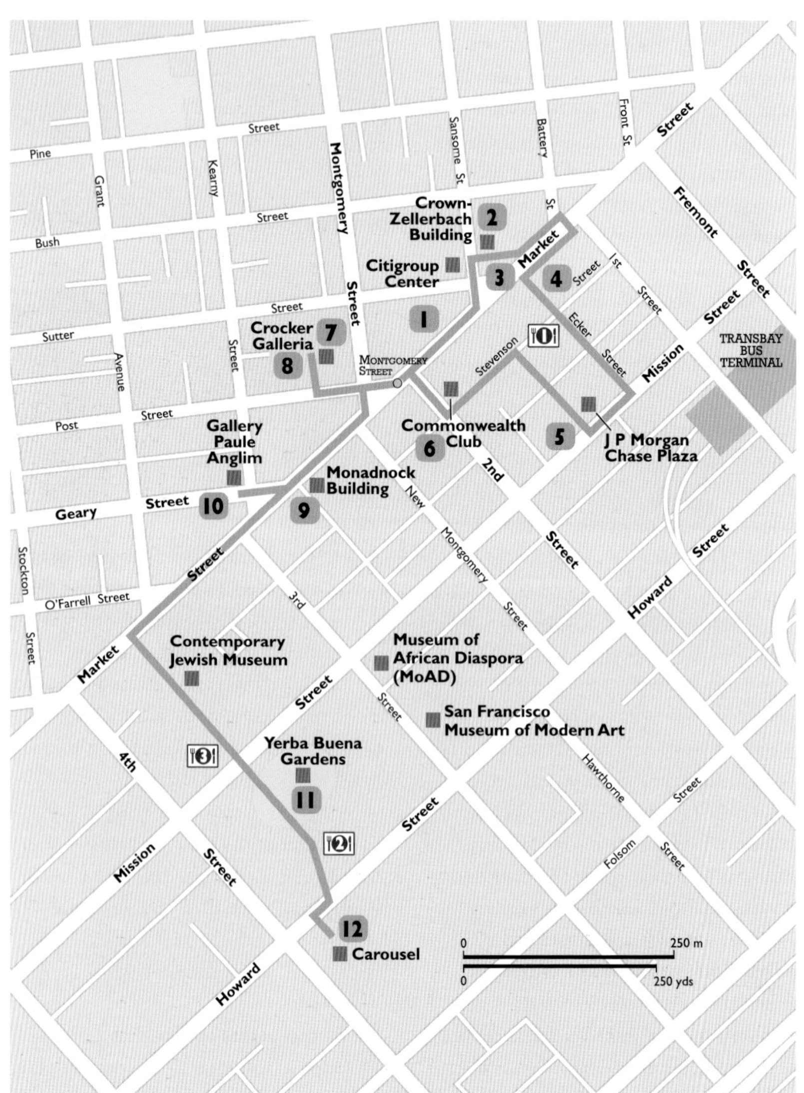

this moment of tranquillity along old alleyways? Continue on Ecker (a brick pathway). At Mission Street, turn right to J P Morgan Chase Plaza, 560 Mission.

The kinetic sculpture reflecting pool and bamboo garden do much to soften the glass, steel and granite surrounding them. A tranquil spot.

5 Continue to the rear of the park, cross Jessie Street to the fountain, and pass through the small plaza next to Neeto's cafe, 71 Stevenson Street. Turn left on Stevenson to 2nd Street.

The open space here has been converted into cafe seating – it's nice but some people are uncomfortable about the lack of public access, as most of the space is for cafe customers' use only. Look up 2nd Street across Market to the mustard-gold Hobart Building, a 1914 design by the prolific, talented and cantankerous architect Willis Polk (1867-1924). Its now-dwarfed tower is still a delight to the eye. (More on Polk in a minute.)

6 Turn right on 2nd Street to Market Street and cross. Veer left on Post Street, walk past the Wells Fargo Bank, and enter the Crocker Galleria. Take the escalators up to the top floor, and turn right and follow the corridor to the back. Go through the doors and climb a flight of stairs to the Roof Terrace.

Looking at the polished surfaces that shoot skyward around you, it's easy to imagine how bleak the city would be without little gardens like this one. Before retracing your steps out of the Roof Garden, look across the street below and notice the building just to your right (130-150 Sutter Street). This is another Willis Polk creation. Called the Hallidie Building (for Andrew Hallidie, 1836-1900, the inventor of the cable car), it was revolutionary for its time – 1917 – because of its glass "curtain wall". Polk wanted to emphasize how the interior steel beams hold up the building, not the exterior walls, so he made the walls out of glass.

7 Exit the staircase from the Roof Terrace, cross to the other side of the Galleria, and turn right along the corridor to the mid-point. Turn in left at

WHERE TO EAT

1 YANK SING,
49 Stevenson Street at Ecker;
Tel: 1-415-541-4949.
A popular lunchtime spot with a good variety of dim sum. $$

2 SAMOVAR IN YERBA BUENA GARDENS,
730 Howard Street;
Tel: 1-415-227-9400.
Exotic teas, snacks and tea-based meals. $$

3 BEARD PAPA'S,
99 Yerba Buena Lane at Mission Street;
Tel: 1-415-978-9972.
Cream puffs, éclairs and popovers – great when they're hot. Very popular! $

the stairway marked Roof Garden and climb these stairs.

A few years ago, this was the third floor of a 12-storey tower. Then the owner reduced the tower and created the roof-top garden here, while at the same time building the even taller high-rise block next door.

8 Backtrack to ground level (or take the elevator down, and exit through the bank). Cross Market Street, and turn right. Enter the Monadnock Building at 685 Market Street. Sign in with Security and go up to the Modernism Gallery on the second floor.

This smallish museum provides a peaceful respite from the hustle and bustle of Market Street, which can be seen from its windows. A hundred years ago, this intersection was media central, home to the offices of all the city's major daily newspapers: *The Chronicle* (de Young Building), the *Examiner* (Hearst Building) and the *Call* (now, Central Tower).

The de Young Building, which was the city's first skyscraper (1899), has recently received a facelift and reopened as an upmarket condominium block. The odd-looking monument on the island in the street is Lotta's Fountain, a gift to the city from Lotta Crabtree, a little red-haired gold-rush girl who entertained gold miners with her song and dance routines and went on to stage success.

MODERNISM GALLERY;
685 MARKET STREET; www.modernisminc.com

9 As you exit the Monadnock Building, turn left. Cross Market Street and then over to Geary Street, which angles off to the left. On the right, at 14 Geary, enter Gallery Paule Anglim.

The constantly changing exhibits at this even smaller gallery are worth a look.

GALLERY PAULE ANGLIM;
14 GEARY STREET; www.gallerypauleanglim.com

10 Return to Market Street, cross, and continue to where the pavement becomes a wide plaza at Yerba Buena Lane. Turn left and continue past the Contemporary Jewish Museum through to Yerba Buena Gardens.

Decades of wrangling over development rules and regulations preceded the creation of these gardens. They are now a centre for the arts and a magnet for independent museums, hotels, restaurants, and lots and lots of city dwellers. Among the nearby museums are:

SAN FRANCISCO MUSEUM OF MODERN ART;
www.sfmoma.org

CONTEMPORARY JEWISH MUSEUM;
www.jmsf.org

CARTOON ART MUSEUM;
www.cartoonart.org

CALIFORNIA HISTORICAL SOCIETY;
www.californiahistoricalsociety.org

MUSEUM OF THE AFRICAN DIASPORA;
www.moadsf.org

GLBT HISTORICAL SOCIETY MUSEUM;
www.glbthistory.org

SOCIETY OF CALIFORNIA PIONEERS;
www.californiapioneers.org

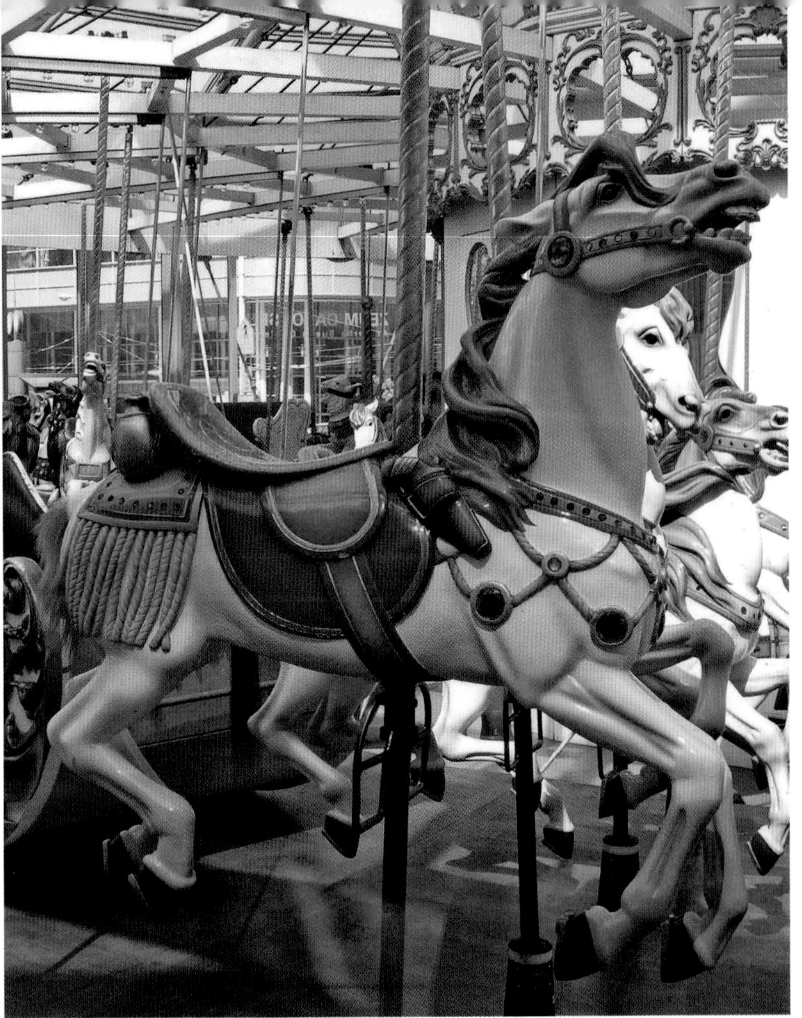

11 **At the back of the first level of the gardens, walk behind the fountain at the Martin Luther King Jr memorial. Then take the stairs above the memorial and continue to the upper level and across the footbridge to the carousel.**

Originally made for San Francisco by German carousel builder Charles Looff (1852–1918), the carousel was en route to the city in 1906 when the earthquake hit and it was diverted to Seattle. It did come to San Francisco, then was moved 60 years later to Los Angeles. Recently it returned for rehabilitation.

12 **Backtrack through the gardens and Yerba Buena Lane to Market Street. You're half way between Powell and Montgomery Muni/BART stops.**

ABOVE: THE BEAUTIFUL HAND-CARVED CAROUSEL IN YERBA BUENA GARDENS

WALK 6

Chinatown – a City within the City

A walk through the city's exotic alleys will take you past hanging lanterns, Protestant missions, Buddhist temples and fortune-cookie factories.

Chinatown is an exotic and vibrant "city within a city", a thriving, densely packed residential community. It is an active shopping centre, offering Asian foods, medicines and housewares not available elsewhere, as well as a tourist centre. The first Chinese immigrants maintained their traditions, expecting only a brief stay in "Gold Mountain". Their manpower was essential in mining and building railroads, but with an economic downturn in the 1870s, Chinese immigrants became the target of other workers' anger, distrust and even violence. Immigration laws were changed to limit newcomers from China, and Chinatown was constrained by law and custom to a six-block area. Organizations of mutual support provided aid within the community, and helped mediate disputes both inside Chinatown and with the world outside. In the 19th century, tourists were fascinated by the exotic people they called "celestials", with their funny shoes and long pigtails – and also by opium dens, "high-binders" (gangsters), prostitutes and depravity. The vice is now gone but the attraction is still powerful.

1 Start at Chinatown Gates, where Grant Avenue meets Bush Street. (Walk up from either Montgomery St or Powell Muni/BART station and cut over to Grant.) Go north along Grant.

Right away you'll notice a faster pace and more crowded feeling. Listen for the sounds of the man playing the two-string erhu. Look up at the buildings. The basic architecture is standard post-1906, but the embellishments are definitely Chinatown (but not Chinese): bright balconies, hanging lanterns or pagoda-like eaves. Stop at the corner of Grant and Sacramento Street.

Across the street, at 736 Grant, *The Chinese World Newspaper*, the first Chinese-owned bilingual Chinese and English daily in the US, was published here in 1909-69. There's a banner on the upstairs balcony. Bank of America, 701 Grant, has a gold mosaic façade typical of the kind of decoration large corporations add to make local branches feel at home in Chinatown. Upstairs from Bank of America is the Gold Mountain Sagely Monastery, 800 Sacramento, run by the Dharma Realm Buddhist Association for monks and others who come to chant and pray. There's a friendly welcome and selection of booklets inside.

2 Turn left uphill on Sacramento Street. At Waverly, pass the Chinatown YMCA, and the First Chinese Baptist Church (since 1880). Continuing on past Stockton Street, on your right is the red brick Donaldina Cameron House, 920 Sacramento.

WHERE TO EAT

1 GOLDEN GATE FORTUNE COOKIE FACTORY,
56 Ross Alley;
Tel: 1-415-781-3956.
Buy a bag of almond or fortune cookies and they'll give you a few extras hot off the presses. $

2 GOLD MOUNTAIN,
644 Broadway (near Stockton);
Tel: 1-415-296-7733.
Large restaurant with good dim sum. $$

3 EASTERN BAKERY,
720 Grant Avenue (near Commercial);
Tel: 1-415-982-5157.
Nice selection of pastries. The steamed pork buns are excellent. $

Donaldina Cameron was a young woman when she arrived in Chinatown in 1895, planning to work for one year teaching sewing at the Presbyterian Occidental Mission Home for Girls. What she discovered was that prostitution was flourishing. By the time she left 40 years later, she had helped rescue more than 3,000 Chinese girls who had been sold into slavery as prostitutes. Imagine this woman in her later years wielding a crowbar or an axe, scuttling up fire escapes and over rooftops, to break in through false ceilings and rescue frightened teenagers. A mural of her exploits graces the inside lobby.

OPPOSITE: EXOTIC PRODUCE AT A CHINATOWN STREET MARKET

DISTANCE 1.5 miles (2.5km)

ALLOW 2 hours

START Grant Avenue at Bush Street

FINISH California Street cable car

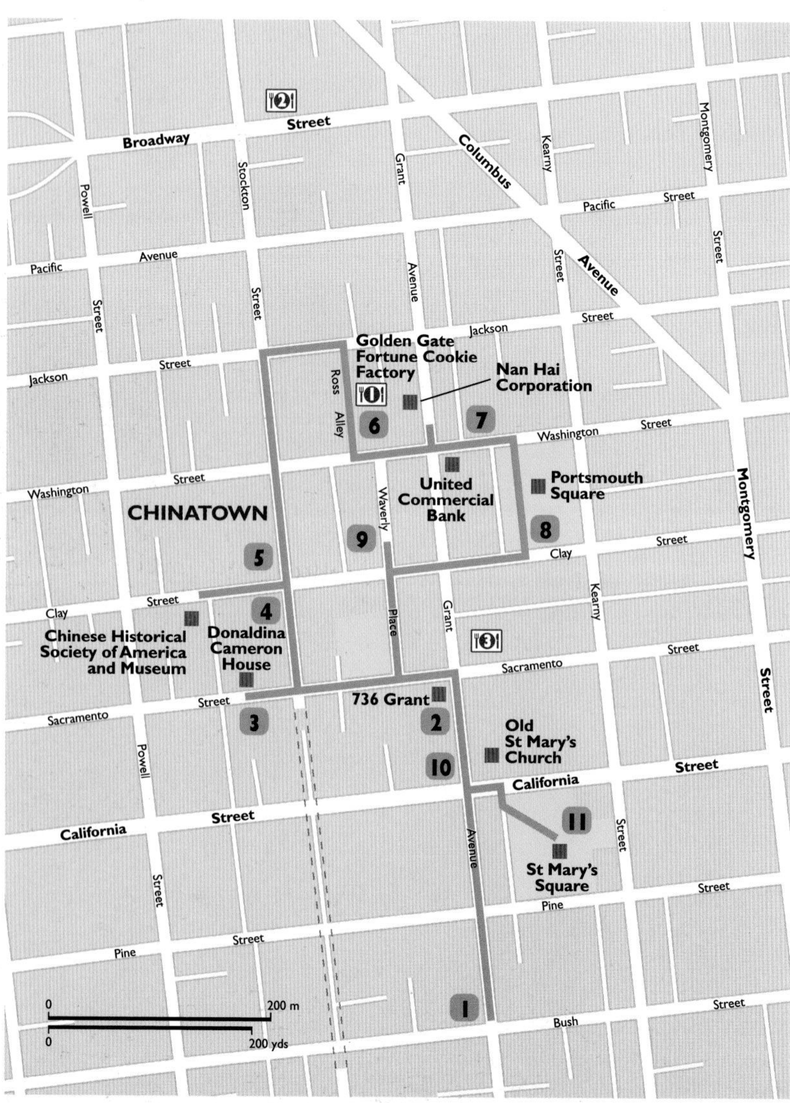

OPPOSITE: A MUSICAL INTERLUDE IN CHINATOWN

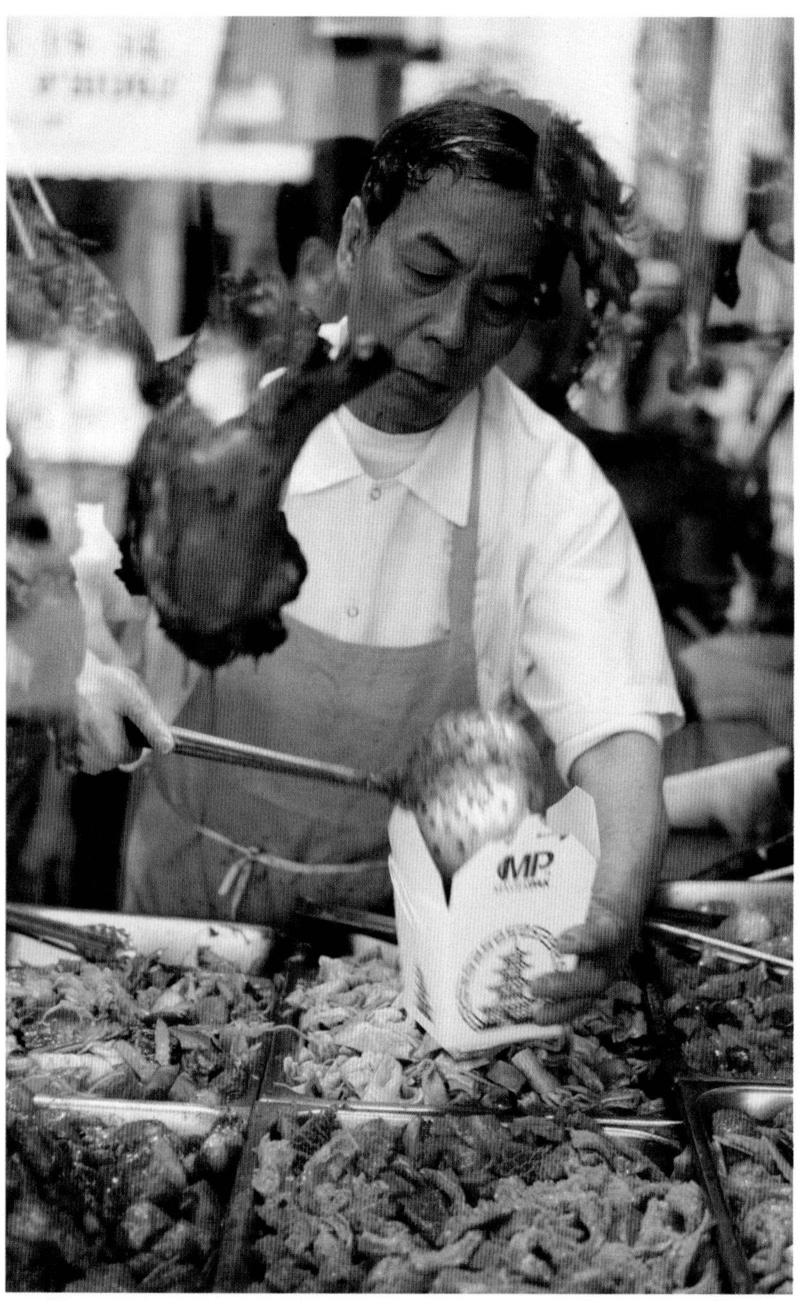

ABOVE: FAST FOOD CHINESE STYLE

3 Backtrack down to Stockton and turn left. This block is Chinatown's "civic centre", with the Chinese Central High School at 829 Stockton, and at 843 Stockton, the Chinese Consolidated Benevolent Society ("Six Companies"), the 1870s mutual aid organization.

At 855 Stockton, a four-storey building houses a post office, travel agencies, medical offices and, on the top floor, the Kong Chow Temple. The original temple, built in 1857, was displaced by a car park. The new location seems incongruous, but as you exit the elevator, with the air suddenly heavy with incense, you see the brilliantly coloured altars and the view out over the rooftops, and know you've been transported to the land of celestials.

4 At Clay Street, turn left uphill to 965 Clay, the Chinese Historical Society of America and Museum with exhibits depicting the Chinese experience in the US. Backtrack down Clay, then turn left on Stockton.

While Grant Avenue (where the walk began) is the shopping area for jewellery, housewares and souvenirs, Stockton is the poultry, fish and produce mall – where Chinese-Americans come to buy bok choi, smoked duck and live fish.

CHINESE HISTORICAL SOCIETY OF AMERICA AND MUSEUM;
965 CLAY STREET; www.chsa.org

5 Pass the Chinese Presbyterian Church at 925 Stockton (Donaldina Cameron's church). At Jackson Street, turn right downhill to Ross Alley. Turn right again on Ross Alley. Just up on the left past the barber shop is the Golden Gate Fortune Cookie Factory, 56 Ross Alley.

Watch the women work the presses. Someone will probably offer you a hot cookie to try, especially if you purchase a small bag to take away. Ross Alley has a shady past; in the 19th century it was a haven for gamblers and the high-binders who controlled prostitutes. Now, Chinatown's alleyways serve a different purpose, providing short-cuts for pedestrians.

6 Continue to the end of Ross Alley. Turn left on Washington Street. At Grant Avenue, it's well worth a quick detour a few doors left to Nan Hai Corporation (919 Grant) with its amazing assortment of dried fish, herbs, ginseng, berries and untold more. Back on Washington, just past Grant, look for the small building on the right with colourful triple roofs (United Commercial Bank). It was once the Telephone Exchange, 743 Washington.

Before automated dialling equipment (introduced in 1949), 20 switchboard operators here connected all calls inside Chinatown; they spoke the five local Chinese dialects, and English too, and knew thousands of residents by name, address and phone number.

7 Continue walking on, then turn right into Portsmouth Square.

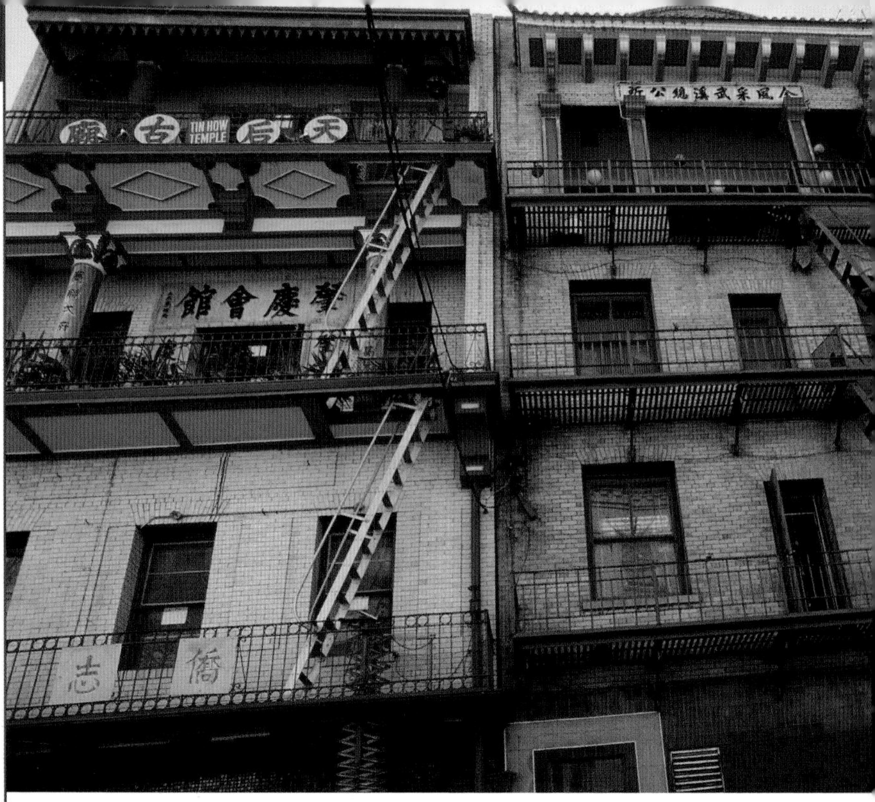

When San Francisco was still called Yerba Buena, and California belonged to Mexico, this was the original plaza. When Yerba Buena became San Francisco, and California was transferred to the US, the old plaza continued as town centre. Now it is a gathering spot for Chinese-Americans, with clusters of men playing, watching and commenting on board games, and clusters of women playing cards, chatting and tending babies.

From Portsmouth Square, if you look back out at Washington Street, you'll notice the big, modern building at the corner (720 Washington), which is Buddha's Universal Church. Replacing a nightclub that had been on this site, the church was built in 1961 by members of the strongly Americanized Pristine Orthodox Dharma. If you're feeling tired, visit the corner store below Buddha's Universal Church: the World Ginseng Center, 801 Kearny, offers many forms of ginseng and other health products.

BUDDHA'S UNIVERSAL CHURCH;
720 WASHINGTON STREET; www.bucsf.com

8 Exit Portsmouth Square opposite where you entered, on Clay Street. Turn right (uphill) on Clay past Grant to Waverly Place. Turn right into Waverly.

Long ago, Waverly was a tough street, reputedly frequented by prostitutes,

ABOVE: THE TINY TIN HOW TEMPLE ON THE TOP FLOOR OF THE BUILDING ON THE LEFT

pimps, gamblers and other petty criminals, and with 40 or 50 houses of ill repute along its two-block length. The corner of Clay and Waverly is the spot where "Little Pete" (Fong Ching) – the most powerful racketeer in Chinatown – was gunned down in 1897. His assailants were never caught.

None of the old edginess is palpable these days. Instead, the atmosphere is bright, cheery and colourful. It's worth a climb (three flights) to the venerable Tin How Temple, 125 Waverly Place, said to be the oldest Chinese temple in the US. You can light a stick of incense and pray to the Queen of the Heavens and the Protector of Travellers.

9 Backtrack along Waverly to Sacramento, where Waverly ends. Dragon costumes (for New Years parades), and Chinese and other exotic musical instruments are for sale at the corner store: Clarion Music Center. Turn left downhill on Sacramento, then turn right on Grant Avenue to Old St Mary's Church.

The only major Chinatown structure to survive 1906, this former cathedral was built of bricks brought from China in the 1850s. Note the plaque on the front wall, the historic photos just inside and the admonition on the bell tower: "Son, Observe the time and fly from Evil."
CLARION MUSIC CENTER;
816 SACRAMENTO STREET;
www.clarionmusic.com

10 Walk – don't fly – across California Street to the park, St Mary's Square.

Sculptor Benny Bufano's (1898-1970) statue of Sun Yat-Sen, the "Father of Modern China" (1866-1925), reminds us that many different waves of immigrants came from China, some drawn by the gold California had to offer, some pushed away by political or economic struggles in their place of birth.

11 Backtrack out of St Mary's Square to California Street, where you can catch a cable car, or turn left on Grant Avenue to walk down to the Chinatown gates at Bush Street, where you started this walk.

WALK 7

On the Beat Trail in North Beach

North Beach used to be the Latin Quarter. Now it's sometimes known as Little Italy. It was home to the Beats. One thing it is not is a beach!

In the 1850s, North Beach bordered the lively (and often down-and-out) waterfront district called the Barbary Coast (see Walk 2). When ships crowded in, poor immigrants from relatively nearby ports in Chile, Peru and Mexico built their make-shift tents and shacks on the muddy slopes that no one else was willing to climb. Waves of Italian fishermen showed up in the late 19th century, as you will see when you visit the North Beach Museum. By the middle of the 20th century, North Beach gained fame as home to the Beat culture (a visit to the Beat Museum will explain all). After 13 October 1955 – when Allen Ginsberg (1926-97) read his poem *Howl,* City Lights bookstore published it, and the government banned it – more poets and wannabees flooded San Francisco in search of freedom. Comedian Lenny Bruce (1925-66) performed – and was busted – here. Sixties icon Carol Doda danced topless. This is a walk that works either during the day or at night. The cafes, restaurants and clubs are great.

Take the Muni bus No. 9X, 41 or 45 to Washington Square.

This is one of two parks (along with Union Square) for which space was set aside in the original town survey. For months after the fires of 1906, it was a refugee camp for unhoused locals. If you're here by 9am you'll see tai chi and other practitioners limbering up (nearby Chinatown has spread into this formerly Italian-only neighbourhood).

If you get here after the tai chi enthusiasts have left, stop by the cement bench in the park near the corner of Stockton Street and Filbert Street. Its plaque commemorates Juana Briones, an early businesswoman, landowner, mother and healer. In 1835, she legally separated from an abusive husband, and took title to land in and around what is now Washington Square. She tended sick soldiers, worked as a midwife, healer of scurvy patients and bonesetter; and in her free time she tended a vast garden, raised dairy cows, and sold milk and vegetables. You could also visit Saints Peter and Paul Church (1924), originally the parish church for local Italian fishermen, which dominates the square.

2 Exit Washington Square at Union Street and Columbus Avenue, turning uphill on Columbus. Turn right at Green Street (aka Beach Blanket Babylon Street), and walk up to Club Fugazi, 678 Green.

In the 1950s, poetry readings were held in this hall. Since the 1970s, it has been home to the ever-changing, outrageous musical revue, *Beach Blanket Babylon*

CLUB FUGAZI;

678 GREEN STREET;

www.beachblanketbabylon.com.

WHERE TO EAT

1 LIGURIA BAKERY,
1700 Stockton Street (across from the park at Filbert Street);
Tel: 1-415-421-3786.
Selling only focaccia, this popular bakery closes each day when they run out of bread. $

green onion focaccia

2 STINKING ROSE,
325 Columbus Avenue;
Tel: 1-415-781-7673.
A self-described garlic restaurant. $$

3 CAFFE PUCCINI,
411 Columbus Avenue;
Tel: 1-415-989-7033.
A good place for sandwiches and soup. $

3 Backtrack to Columbus, turn right on Stockton Street and go into the US Bank that houses the North Beach Museum, upstairs at 1435 Stockton.

The museum has a good selection of historic photographs of the district. You might also spot a foghorn, boxing gloves, an accordion, a mandolin and antique cameras. Open banker's hours: usually Mon-Fri 8-5, Sat 10-12.

OPPOSITE: CITY LIGHTS BOOKSTORE, HAVEN OF ALTERNATIVE CULTURE

DISTANCE **1 mile (1.6km)**

ALLOW **2 hours**

START **Washington Square**

FINISH **Washington Square**

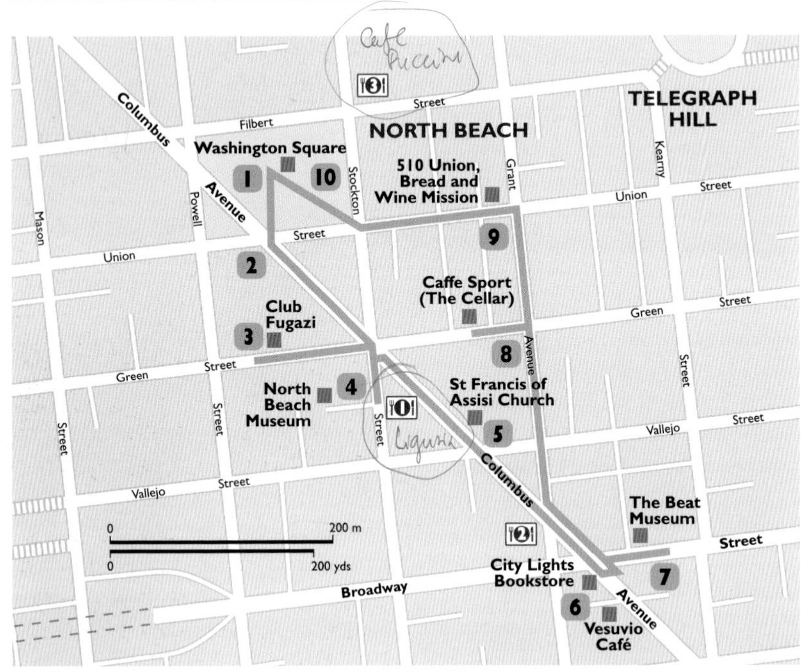

4 Backtrack and continue down Columbus to Vallejo Street. Note the tiny, nondescript alley named for the spiritual father of Beat-era poets, Kenneth Rexroth (1905-82). Then cross Columbus to St Francis of Assisi Church, 610 Vallejo.

St Francis of Assisi Church, North Beach's oldest church, was established in 1849. No longer a parish church, it is now run by the Franciscan Order. Free Sunday concerts are held.

ST FRANCIS OF ASSISI CHURCH;
610 VALLEJO STREET;
www.shrinesf.org/history.htm

5 Continue on Columbus Avenue. Cross Broadway to City Lights bookstore, 261 Columbus.

City Lights is ground-zero for Beat culture. Peter Martin and Lawrence Ferlinghetti started it as an all-paperback bookstore in 1953. (Martin hoped for an income stream to pay rent for his magazine publishing office upstairs; Ferlinghetti wanted to create a literary meeting place.) Martin soon left and Ferlinghetti stayed on, expanding the store over time and also adding a publishing house, made famous during the obscenity trial over the publication of Ginsberg's *Howl and Other Poems* (City Lights, 1956). Half a century later, Ferlinghetti and City Lights still nurture and encourage North Beach's vibrancy and tolerance.

Just below City Lights is Jack Kerouac Alley, named for the author (1922-69) of *On the Road* (called "the essence, history, myth of the Beat Generation"), *Visions of Cody* and *Doctor Sax*. Twice a year there's an art festival here. The walls are painted with murals, and poetry is embedded in the walkway plaques. Facing onto the alley is the Vesuvio Café, a hang-out popular with Kerouac and other Beat poets. Now, their clientele includes artists, chess players, cab drivers, seamen, business people, European visitors, off-duty exotic dancers and *bons vivants* from all walks of life.

Look across the street. Here, the continuation of Jack Kerouac Alley is called William Saroyan Alley after the writer (1908-81). Spec's pub is home to the Adler Museum – really a collection of photos on the walls. This is a friendly place, open only in the evenings.

Look down Columbus Avenue and you can't miss the Transamerica Pyramid that now sits on the site of the old Montgomery Block (1853-1959). Built in the gold-rush era, the venerable old building was sufficiently run down in its later years that rooms were let at

affordable prices to struggling writers and artists. The young poet Kenneth Rexroth (1905-82) lived here for a time. (Rexroth called San Francisco a haven for thinking, feeling people.)

VESUVIO CAFÉ;

255 COLUMBUS AVENUE; www.vesuvio.com

6 Backtrack on Columbus Avenue, cross and then turn right on Broadway Street, and cross to 540 Broadway, the Beat Museum.

This is the place to learn about Beat culture. Wander into the front, and buy cheap paperbacks ("bathtub literature"), first editions signed by the author, t-shirts or a poster featuring Ginsberg's *Howl*. $5 buys entrance to this time capsule of early

ABOVE: VESUVIO CAFÉ, POPULAR WITH THE BEAT POETS OF THE 1950s

manuscripts, news clippings, photos, old typewriters and other memorabilia.

Outside the museum, this stretch of Broadway, on either side of Columbus, is an odd mix of sleazy, upscale and historical. The Condor nightclub at the corner was made famous when former waitress and Sixties icon Carol Doda first danced topless (and later, bottomless) here.

The mural on the building across the street (606 Broadway) celebrates music, politicians and North Beach life.

THE BEAT MUSEUM;
540 BROADWAY STREET;
www.thebeatmuseum.org

7 Backtrack on Broadway, veer right uphill on Columbus, then right uphill on Grant Avenue. The next blocks were home to many Beat hang-outs, including:

Café Trieste, 609 Vallejo. Still a popular, family-run cafe, this was a favourite with the Beats. Later, Francis Ford Coppola is said to have written some of *The Godfather* here while nursing numerous stimulating espressos.

No longer here, the one-time Coffee Gallery at 1353 Grant, along with The Cellar (see right), was a place where performances of Beat music were common. What's Beat music? Guitar, washboard, piano or other music, not unlike jazz, accompanied by a performance of spoken poetry. Another Beat hang-out, the Co-existence Bagel shop, 1398 Grant (on the corner of Green) has been replaced by a trendy Thai restaurant. Note that bagels are a speciality of New York, not San Francisco; many of the Beat poets who took up residence in San Francisco were originally New Yorkers (Allen Ginsberg, Gregory Corso, Peter Orlovsky and Jack Kerouac). Across the street (1371 Grant) is Grant & Green Saloon – not a Beat hang-out but they do have live music.

8 Turn left on Green Street. At 576 Green, what is now Caffe Sport was The Cellar, a major venue for the Beats in the 1950s. Backtrack up Green Street to Grant Avenue. Turn left.

The other side of Grant, on the left, is the Bocce Caffe, 480 Green, with a delightful garden path-entry to the restaurant. Grant Avenue has small avant-garde art galleries such as Live Worms at 1345 Grant and I Dream of Cake at 1351 Grant.

9 At Union Street, turn left, downhill.

On the right is 510 Union, one of the homes of the Bread and Wine Mission. The brainchild of liberal Congregational minister Pierre Delattre, this was a gathering place for itinerant poets. Occasionally – when a local poet got the urge to put it together – the *Beatitude* magazine was published at Bread and Wine. On the left, Via Ferlinghetti (formerly Price Row) is small and undistinguished, especially in comparison to its namesake Lawrence Ferlinghetti who has been so pivotal to this area.

10 End back in Washington Square.

OPPOSITE: A MURAL ON COLUMBUS AND GRANT, CELEBRATING THE CITY'S MUSIC

THE CASTLE HOTEL
-ELI-
DOUGHERT
TONY KLAAS

WALK

8 Firemen and Views from Telegraph Hill

From telegraph to TV, blue jeans to cherry-headed parrots, and a little girl who fell in love with firemen, this is a great walk at the edge of downtown.

In a city of hills, Telegraph Hill stands out. Called Loma Alta (Tall Hill), then Prospect Hill and now Telegraph Hill – by any name, this is a spectacular hill at the edge of the bay. Some of the slopes were so steep, early residents needed ladders to get up and down. And, at a time when men outnumbered women 50:1, the arrival of members of the fairer sex was a newsworthy event announced by semaphore from the hilltop. Later, after Guglielmo Marconi (1874–1937) invented his wireless telegraphy system, messages could be sent from here to the city's Land's End district and beyond (see Walk 24). On this walk, you'll pass through districts that the rich didn't bother with until the 1930s. You'll catch unsurpassed views across the bay. You'll see socially conscious murals lining the walls inside a nozzle-shaped fire tower, smell eucalyptus, hear parrots, be amused by vehicles trying to negotiate steep narrow streets, and then descend a magical staircase to the edge of the old port where you can relax in a new park.

1 Take the No. 39 Muni bus to the top of Telegraph Hill – or walk there.

Start by visiting Coit Tower. Inside, signs explain the 1930s murals that cover the walls.

Eccentric Lillie Hitchcock Coit (1842-1929) married money, travelled widely and had a special fondness for firemen. When she died, she left one-third of her considerable fortune to the city, "to be expended in an appropriate manner for the purpose of adding to the beauty of the city which I have always loved". After some consideration, the executors of her will built a monument for firemen in Washington Square, and Coit Tower. As the story goes, little Lillie Hitchcock was only eight when firemen saved her from a burning building. A few years later, coming home from school one afternoon, she saw the Knickerbocker Fire Engine No. 5 volunteers struggling to pull the engine up the slopes of Telegraph Hill. Little Lillie took the engine's extra rope and pulled, and called on passersby to help. (These were the days when volunteers manned fire engines and competed for the glory of putting out a fire.) Forever after, Knickerbocker loved Lillie, and she loved them.

2 Leaving the tower, walk along the pathway next to the road, and turn left down the Greenwich Street stairs. Turn left at the first road (Montgomery Street) to the end of the road.

This is the entrance to Julius Castle restaurant, the fantasy of Italian

immigrant and restaurant worker Julius Roz. Built to look like a castle when seen from ships and boats looking up from the bay, the restaurant is actually made of redwood and maple, not granite and marble.

3 Backtrack along Montgomery Street to Union Street. At the corner on the left is a very old set of flats: 1252, 1254-1256 Montgomery. Walk a little farther along Montgomery to where the road ends.

The flats date from the 1860s, when this area was accessible only on foot – and sometimes by ladder. The steepness was a boon in 1906, when rock outcroppings served as a natural firebreak – probably the reason these buildings survived the great fire. (The stories that residents poured wine on the fires to douse them are apocryphal.)

OPPOSITE: COIT TOWER MURAL; ABOVE: MONUMENT TO THE CITY'S FIREMEN IN WASHINGTON SQUARE

DISTANCE **1 mile (1.6km) – some steep downhill stairs**

ALLOW **1-1.5 hours**

START **Top of Telegraph Hill**

FINISH **The Embarcadero**

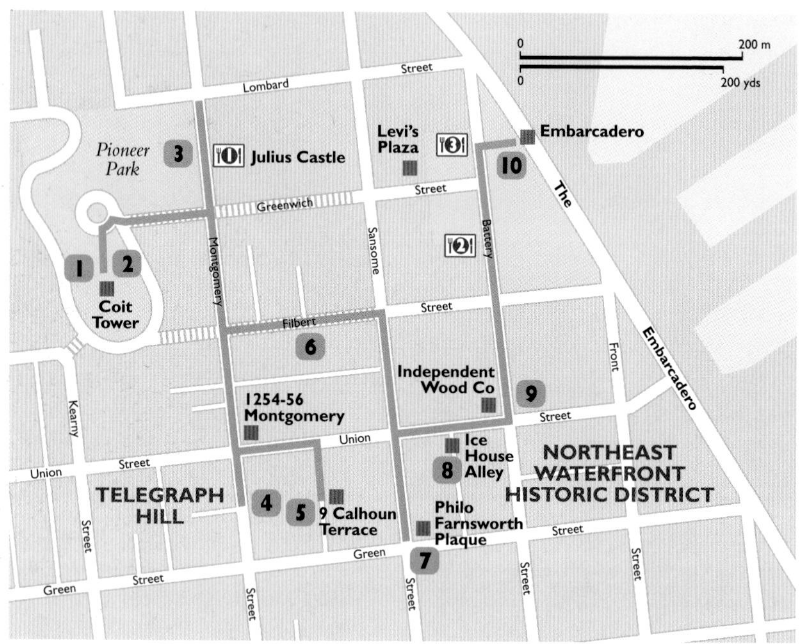

Proximity to the bustling port below was the principal reason to live here. During the gold rush, this area was known as Little Chile, for the workers – sailors, dockworkers and prostitutes – who arrived from the relatively nearby ports of Chile, Peru, Panama and Mexico. (In those days, the fastest way to get to California was by ship.) Homes were built from materials salvaged from abandoned ships in the harbour – wood was turned into shacks, and sails into tents. As the city grew up and the water's edge moved out, this remained a working-class district until recent years.

4 Backtrack along Montgomery to Union Street. Turn right, then right again to 9 Calhoun Terrace.

Like the houses on Montgomery, this carpenter-gothic-style house dates from San Francisco's early days. The original occupant was Dr David G "Yankee" Robinson, a 19th-century physician, comedian and theatre impresario.

OPPOSITE: JULIUS CASTLE RESTAURANT, BUILT TO LOOK LIKE A CASTLE, WITH STUNNING VIEWS OVER THE BAY

5 Backtrack via Calhoun Terrace and Union to Montgomery. Turn right on Montgomery and then turn right down the Filbert Street Steps.

You've probably already heard their calls overhead, but this is the real home of the flock of cherry-headed conures known as the Wild Parrots of Telegraph Hill. They were made famous by local resident Mark Bittner, who has tenaciously studied, protected and loved them for years. (For information on his book and the documentary about them, see www.markbittner.net/parrots_central.html.)

Already steep by nature, this slope of Telegraph Hill was made even more precipitous thanks to intensive rock quarrying. Early quarries provided ballast for outgoing ships. Later they provided rock for grading and paving city streets. The quarry companies – most notoriously the Gray Brothers – had many mighty (and well-rewarded) friends at City Hall, who ignored residents' complaints of noise and disruption. In fact, it was company policy to make local living conditions unbearable, so that the company could purchase lots at bargain prices to hold for future profitable sales. In June 1884, one particularly ferocious blast set off landslides that demolished houses on Calhoun Terrace and elsewhere. When the Gray Brothers openly defied a court injunction to stop blasting, Telegraph Hill residents protested by throwing rocks on the Gray Brothers' works below. The locals weren't the only people the Gray brothers treated badly. In 1915, a disgruntled employee shot and killed one of the brothers. After this, the blasting finally stopped.

6 Enjoy the walk to the bottom of the stairway. Turn right on Sansome Street. Two blocks down, find the plaque at 200 Green commemorating Philo Taylor Farnsworth.

Philo Farnsworth (1906-71) was 22 when he announced his all-electronic television system in 1927. The Utah-born Mormon

ABOVE: ONE OF THE STEEP AND SPECTACULAR STREETS ON THE EDGE OF THE BAY

farm boy had developed the concept as a high-school science project. When RCA started using his technology, he fought them for patent infringement and won.

7 Backtrack on Sansome to Union Street and turn right. Stop at Ice House Alley to admire the mix of old and new buildings.

After their downtown offices were destroyed in 1906, the *San Francisco Bulletin* newspaper found temporary quarters in the Merchant's Ice Company, at the northern end of Sansome Street, by the foot of the Telegraph Hill cliffs. Editorial and linotype rooms were on the roof, and the pressroom was in a shack on the ground below.

8 Continue on Union, then turn left on Battery Street. Stop at 1105 Battery at Union.

This is the old Independent Wood Co building. A typical layout for buildings in the port district, 1105 Battery was designed for retail on ground floor and rooms for seamen above.

9 Continue on Battery Street and wander through Levi's Plaza – a nice intermingling of old and new structures.

German-born 24-year-old Levi Strauss (1829-1902) came to San Francisco in 1853 to open a branch of his brothers' dry goods business. A customer for Levi's cloth was Latvian immigrant Jacob Davis, whose tailoring business created work

WHERE TO EAT

1 JULIUS CASTLE,
1541 Montgomery Street;
Tel: 1-415-392-2222.
Stunning views not let down by the food. $$$

2 FOG CITY DINER,
1300 Battery Street;
Tel: 1-415-982-2000.
Fun, classic diner food with a San Francisco twist. $$

3 IL FORNAIO,
1265 Battery Street;
Tel: 1-415-986-0100.
In Levi's Plaza – delicious take-away or sit-down meals. $$

clothes for miners. He found that miners' pockets, loaded down with tools, gold and silver, kept ripping out. Davis's solution was to apply rivets to the pockets. But Davis couldn't afford to pay the $68 price of a patent, so he went into business with Strauss. From 1873 to 1890, their patent gave them exclusive rights to manufacture and sell riveted-pocket overalls. Under the park here, at about Filbert and Battery, lie the remains of the gold-rush-era storeship *William Grey*, dating from the time that this was bay land.

10 Turn right through the park about half a block to the Embarcadero, to the Muni/BART station, or catch the historic F-line trolley either to the Ferry Building or Fisherman's Wharf.

COIT TOWER, WITH ALCATRAZ BEYOND

WALK 9

Cable Cars, Street Cars, Stage Coaches, Ferries

This walk from Nob Hill through the financial district to the Ferry Building will help you learn about the transit systems so vital to the city.

Historically, San Francisco was connected to the outside world by sea, and overland by stage coach and wagon. The transcontinental railroad opened in 1869, terminating across the bay in Oakland. And the only way across the bay itself was by boat – the bridges weren't built until the 1930s. Within the city, pedestrians, horses, horse-drawn carriages and omnibuses started sharing the cobbled streets in the 1870s with the ingenious new invention – the cable car. Soon, electric street cars – running on tracks like cable cars but powered by overhead wires – started to replace cable cars, which were propelled by gripping an underground cable. Take this walk and sit in a 19th-century stage coach. Listen to the hum of cable car cables and the clang of their bells, and look underground at the machinery that drives them. Gaze across the bay and watch ferry boats come and go. The walk is best on weekdays when all three museums are open: the Cable Car Museum is open every day; Wells Fargo Museum is open weekdays; and the Railway Museum is open Wednesday to Sunday.

1 Take the Hyde Street or Powell Street cable car to the Cable Car Barn and Museum, 1201 Mason Street at Washington Street.

At the historic Ferries & Cliff House Railway Company 1887 Car Barn, solve the mystery of why you hear humming when you walk along Powell or California Street. (Hint: check out the giant spools and cables in the basement.) Learn the magic a gripman knows: when to hold, and when to let go. Ponder how they get the cables – and cable cars – to turn corners.

CABLE CAR BARN AND MUSEUM;
1201 MASON STREET;
www.cablecarmuseum.org/museum.html

2 Walk down Washington Street for one block. Turn right on Powell Street. Turn left (downhill) on Clay to Portsmouth Square.

As you walk down Clay Street, note the steep gradient: you are walking along the route of the first cable car. This is where genius Andrew Hallidie performed his first practical test of the concept of propelling a car by gripping a cable. He thought it would work... but these hills are steep, and no one had ever tried it before. In case the system needed to be adjusted – or worse, if it failed altogether – Hallidie and his backers scheduled their secret test run at 4am on 2 August 1873. If the car jumped the tracks, the streets would be empty and no one would be hurt (or humiliated). But the secret was leaked, the street was packed and, luckily, the system worked.

Cable car accidents are rare but can have surprising consequences. Perhaps the most famous accident happened in 1964 (three years before the Summer of Love, see Walk 18). Gloria Sykes had been in town only two weeks when she took a ride on the Hyde Street cable car. The grip lost its hold on the cable, and the car rushed backwards downhill. There were no serious physical injuries but the psychological trauma to 23-year-old Sykes turned her into a nymphomaniac. She sued for half a million dollars. The jury awarded her $50,000.

3 In the next block, on the left side of Clay Street just before Montgomery, you'll see wall plaques commemorating the historic Pony Express.

For a brief but much-heralded period before telegraph wires were strung between California and the Midwest city of St Joseph, Missouri, the Pony Express provided very fast, very brave riders on specially selected very fast horses, who could relay messages along what had been a 20-day stage coach ride in 10 days. Riders were chosen for their marksmanship, their horsemanship, their bravery, their capacity to endure deprivation, and their weight – under 110 pounds. A 19th-century version of instant messaging.

4 Cross Montgomery, and turn right to Wells Fargo History Museum, 420 Montgomery.

DISTANCE **1.5 miles (2.5km)**

ALLOW **1.5 hours, plus 2 hours at the museums**

START **Cable Car Barn and Museum at the corner of Mason Street and Washington Street**

FINISH **Embarcadero Muni/BART station, or Ferry Building stop on F-Market street car or California Street cable car**

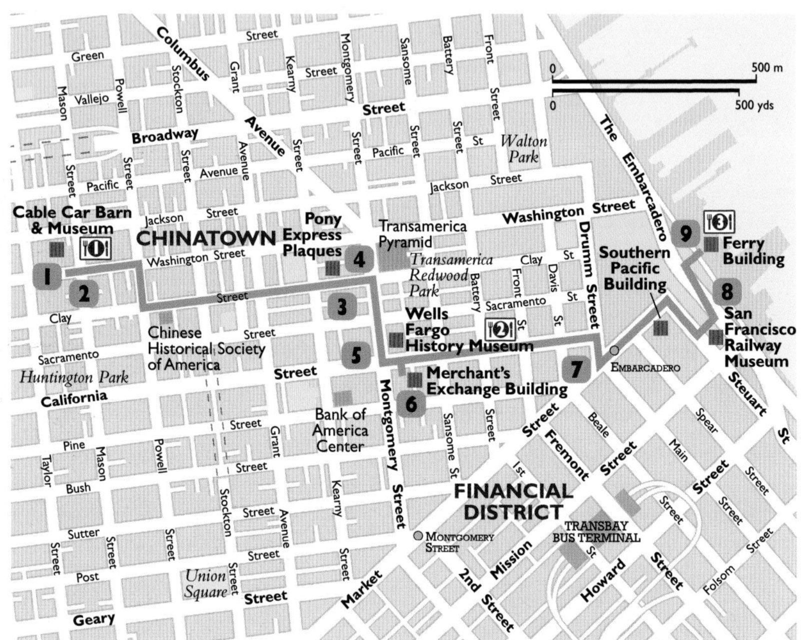

Before planes, trains and automobiles, there was the stage coach. This rich museum offers constantly changing exhibits, from letters and ledger books to gold nuggets and early movies. When you climb in the stage coach, imagine how you might have reacted when Black Bart, the Poet Bandit, held up the stage coach to steal the trunkload of cash.

WELLS FARGO HISTORY MUSEUM;
420 MONTGOMERY STREET;
www.wellsfargohistory.com/museums/museums_sf.htm

5 Leaving the Wells Fargo Museum, turn left to continue on Montgomery Street. Cross California Street, and turn left to the Merchant's Exchange Building, 465 California.

OPPOSITE: CALIFORNIA STREET WITH AN AUTHENTIC CABLE CAR ON THE RIGHT OF THE PICTURE

GW
BAUER'S
LIMO & 17 TRANS.
SERVICE
FOR RESERVATIONS
1-800-LIMO OUT
& Market
STOCKTON
Grant

WHERE TO EAT

①GALLERY CAFÉ,
1200 Mason Street;
Tel: 1-415-296-9932.
For coffee, a sandwich, or a quick pick-me-up after visiting the museum. $

②TADICH GRILL,
240 California Street;
Tel: 1-415-391-1849.
Serving hearty meals since 1849. $$

③LULU PETITE,
Market Place Shop 19, Ferry Building;
Tel: 1-415-362-7019.
One of many good snacking or dining options at the Ferry Building. $$

Walk through to the bank lobby to view the display of Coulter (1839-1946) seascapes.

Irishman William Alexander Coulter's father was captain of the Coast Guard, and at age 13 young William started his own maritime apprenticeship. In off hours at sea, he taught himself to draw and paint. After landing in San Francisco in 1869, he was employed as a sail-maker. On the side, he worked at his art before eventually becoming a full-time artist. His office was around the corner at 325 Montgomery Street. He lived in San Francisco and across the bay in Sausalito for the rest of his life, chronicling the boats and ships in the bay and on the sea.
MERCHANT'S EXCHANGE BUILDING;
465 CALIFORNIA STREET; www.mxbuilding.com

6 Leave the Merchant's Exchange Building and turn right along California Street. Just before Market Street, you'll see cable cars lined up at the California Street terminus.

Notice that there is no turntable here, as there is at either end of the Powell Street lines. Why? Unlike the somewhat smaller cars on the Powell and Hyde Street lines, the California Street cars can go backwards and forwards.

Walk past the end of the car tracks and a few feet to the right. Notice the monument to poet Robert Frost (1874-1963), a San Francisco native.

Now, look across Market Street to the old Southern Pacific Building, at 1 Market Street. For much of the late 19th and early 20th centuries, the Southern Pacific Railroad Company controlled not only the railroads, but also the ferry boats and enormous tracts of land along the rail lines, and had strong tentacles controlling state and local politics and politicians – thus the company moniker, The Octopus.

7 Stay on this side of Market Street and veer left. At the end of Market, cross and walk along Steuart Street, one-half block to the San Francisco Railway Museum, 77 Steuart.

Learn the stories behind the historic, colourful F-line street cars you see along Market Street and the Embarcadero. This small, friendly museum celebrates these cars, painted and restored by volunteers to look like they did when they worked

the streets of Milan, Cleveland, Los Angeles or San Francisco.

SAN FRANCISCO RAILWAY MUSEUM;
77 STEUART STREET; www.streetcar.org

8 When you exit the Railway Museum, cross the plaza in front of you and head to your right, and into the Ferry Building.

In days of yore, what is now the open plaza in front of the Ferry Building was packed with street cars, cable cars, automobiles and pedestrians. The Ferry Building – in this location since 1875 – was the daily corridor through which passengers streamed. Sometimes 120,000 fares were booked in a day. In 1930, 43 ferry boats carried a total of 47 million passengers. (San Francisco's current resident population is about three-quarters of a million.) Where was everyone going? To many points around the bay, Vallejo, San Rafael and Sausalito but most traffic crossed east-west between Oakland and San Francisco. Gertrude Stein, who grew up across the bay in Oakland, is quoted as saying of her hometown: "There is no there, there." Yet, since 1869 when the transcontinental railway's terminus was established there, Oakland's importance has been significant. Until the Bay Bridge (connecting San Francisco and Oakland) and the Golden Gate Bridge opened in the late 1930s, ferry boats were the way most people (and their cars) crossed the bay.

Inside the Ferry Building, if you're not too distracted by the food on offer, check out the historic photo exhibits that line the entry way, and be sure to walk through to the back and sit for a bit watching the ferries come and go.

9 From the Ferry Building, you have several transport options. Directly in front is the historic F-line street car. At Market Street, there's the underground Muni/BART station, or the California Street cable car line.

ABOVE: THE FERRY BUILDING ON THE EMBARCADERO, WITH BAY BRIDGE BEYOND

WALK 10

On Top of the World on Nob Hill

Some call it Snob Hill, but Nob Hill was probably named for the Nabobs, the men of great wealth and importance who built their castles here.

Only the most intrepid lived on these precipitously steep slopes in the 1850s. In the 1870s and 1880s, the rich called it home: shopkeepers who had made a killing in railroads (the "Big Four"), and bartenders who made their money from insider trading and silver mines (the "Bonanza Kings"). After the fires of 1906, the rich built their mansions farther west, and Nob Hill became the place for exclusive men's clubs, fancy pied-a-terre apartments, ritzy hotels and a grand cathedral. In 1945, in the months preceding the founding of the United Nations, formal ceremonies were held down the hill in the Civic Center district (see Walk 12), but the behind-the-scenes negotiations happened here, at the Fairmont and Mark Hopkins hotels. Movie buffs will recognize Nob Hill as the setting for scenes from *Bullitt* (Grace Cathedral, the Pacific Union Club and the Mark Hopkins Hotel), *Vertigo* (Brocklebank Apartments and back streets), and from *Milk* (Grace Cathedral stands in for the church where Dan White went to pray after shooting George Moscone and Harvey Milk).

1 Take the California Street cable car to California and Taylor (Grace Cathedral). Walk up the steps on your right to Grace Cathedral.

Awed by the soaring spires, for a minute before you enter you might think you are in Chartres. Guides inside can explain the history of the cathedral to you. Don't miss the labyrinths (one inside, one outside), and the replica Lorenzo Ghiberti Renaissance front doors.

The cathedral is built on land donated by members of the Crocker family, after their homes were destroyed in 1906. Charles Crocker, one of the Big Four railroad barons, died in 1888; his son William was president of the Crocker National Bank, chair of the 1915 Panama-Pacific International Exposition, and active in community affairs.

GRACE CATHEDRAL;
www.gracecathedral.org

2 Backtrack down the stairs to California Street and cross to the Masonic Auditorium, 1111 California.

It's said that this 1950s lobby and its stained glass wall would be perfectly to scale for 12ft (4m) tall giants. To uncover the secrets of one of the world's oldest and largest fraternal organizations, visit the Henry Wilson Coil Library and Museum of Freemasonry.

HENRY WILSON COIL LIBRARY AND MUSEUM OF FREEMASONRY;
1111 CALIFORNIA STREET;
www.sfmasoniccenter.com/aboutus/building_history.html

3 Continue on California. Turn right (uphill) on Jones Street, then cross and turn left on Sacramento Street. Half way down the block, turn right on Leroy Place to the Water Tank.

Fire Chief Dennis Sullivan was one of the few immediate casualties of the early morning earthquake on 18 April 1906. (The towering chimney of the next-door hotel crashed through the roof of the fire station where he was sleeping.) For years he'd pleaded for better emergency backup systems, but the city couldn't be bothered. It was only after 1906 that funds were freed to implement the policies Sullivan had proposed, including huge hilltop water tanks, like this one, to use gravity to feed a system of pipes with high-pressure water reserved for fighting big fires. (You'll see both fat and skinny water hydrants downtown: the fat ones belong to this separate emergency system.)

OPPOSITE: MARK HOPKINS HOTEL; ABOVE: THE REPLICA RENAISSANCE DOORS OF GRACE CATHEDRAL

DISTANCE **1.3 miles (2.5km)**

ALLOW **1 hour**

START **Grace Cathedral**

FINISH **Powell Street above Union Square**

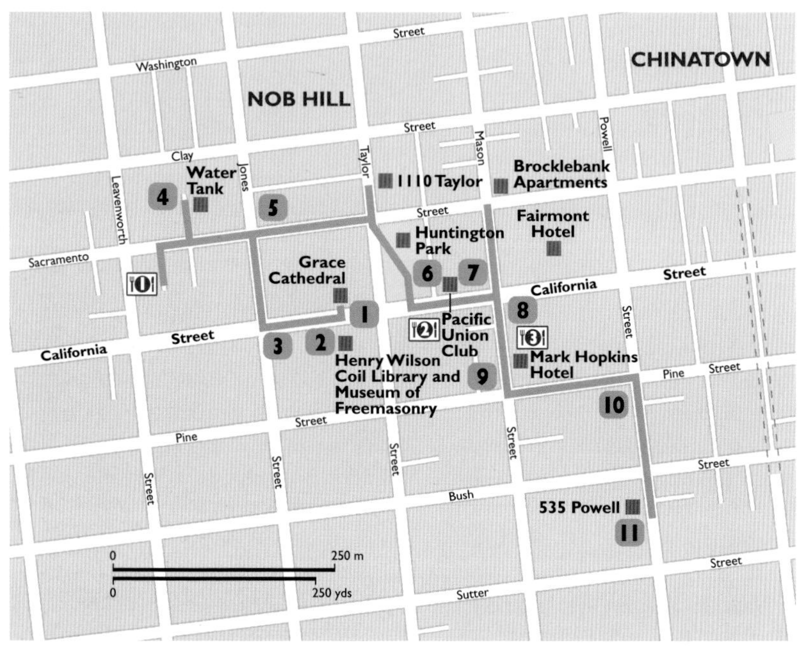

4 Backtrack on Leroy Place to Sacramento Street. Turn right and, in a few feet, check out the tiny Golden Court, across the street. Little alleyways once provided service entrances; now they provide expensive real estate. Backtrack uphill on Sacramento just past Jones.

Where the Cathedral Boys School now stands is the approximate site of Charles Crocker's (1822–88) infamous Spite Fence. Intending to build his Nob Hill mansion on a full block, Crocker bought out all the residents but one, German undertaker Nicolas Yung, who kept raising his asking price until Crocker refused to buy. Crocker built his mansion on the remainder of the block, and at the boundary between their properties, erected a 30ft (9m) high fence (so high that supporting buttresses were required). The fence itself cost $3,000, the price most people would pay for an entire house. Crocker died in 1888, shortly after the fence was erected; Yung died in 1880.

The Yungs had moved to another house they owned (on Broderick Street near Ellis) but refused to sell their lot until mutual heirs came to an agreement in 1904. Two years later, the great 1906 fires consumed the Crocker castle.

5 Continue down Sacramento and turn left on Taylor Street for a few feet to 1110 Taylor. This tiny house, now dwarfed, was originally for the Flood family coachman (see below). Backtrack on Taylor and cross to Huntington Park.

In complicated tales of greed, deceit, high finance and betrayal, this is the site of what was the mansion of David Colton (Southern Pacific Railroad attorney), and later passed to former colleague, then nemesis, Collis Huntington (hardware-store owner turned railroad baron). In 1915, Huntington's widow donated the land to the city.

It is near here that you might spot the ghost of 18-year-old Flora Sommerton, who vanished in 1876 when her parents announced an arranged marriage to a much older man.

6 Exit the other side of the park and turn left on California Street.

The stately brown building on the left is the former Flood Mansion, now the Pacific Union Club. But don't try to enter: this is a private club that never admits visitors or women. Built in 1885 as home to James Flood, the bartender who, acting on overheard remarks and tips from customers, invested cleverly

and made a fortune in Nevada silver mines. It is the only hilltop mansion to have survived the 1906 fires.

7 At Mason Street, cross, and turn left to the corner. At 1000 Mason are the Brocklebank Apartments, made famous when *Vertigo*'s Madeleine lived here and parked her green Jaguar in front. Backtrack to the Fairmont Hotel.

With a planned opening in the summer of 1906 (just a little more interior decoration was needed), the Fairmont Hotel survived the 1906 earthquake, but the interior was gutted by fires sparked by the quake. One year later, on 18 April 1907, the Fairmont finally opened, to exaggerated pronouncements about how the city's recovery was complete. Lovely lobby and corridors with historic photos.

FAIRMONT HOTEL;
www.fairmont.com/sanfrancisco/AboutUs/HotelHistory.htm

ABOVE: LUSH GARDENS ON TINY GOLDEN COURT

WHERE TO EAT

1 CHICO'S MARKET,
1168 Leavenworth;
Tel: 1-415-775-9812.
A long-time favourite with locals for picnic foods and snacks. $

2 THE BIG FOUR RESTAURANT,
The Huntington Hotel,
1075 California Street;
Tel: 1-415-771-1140.
"Men's club" atmosphere; good for lunch. $$$

3 TOP OF THE MARK,
Mark Hopkins Hotel,
California Street at Mason;
Tel: 1-415-616-6916.
Fancy, with fabulous views. $$$

8 Across California Street at Mason is the Mark Hopkins Hotel.

Another of the Big Four railroad barons, Mark Hopkins (1813-78), built his mansion on this site but died before it was completed. After his widow's death, her second husband left the mansion to the San Francisco Art Institute (see Walk 11). In the 1906 quake, many of the paintings were saved but the building was destroyed. The Institute continued to use the site for a modest building, which was torn down in 1926 to be replaced by the current hotel, built by the ambitious young mining engineer and hotel investor George D Smith. Since then, Mick Jagger, Liz Taylor, Elvis, Prince Phillip and the Dalai Lama have all stayed here. There's an interesting little free museum to the right of the lobby.

9 Leaving the Mark Hopkins, turn left (downhill) on Mason Street, then turn left on Pine Street.

The retaining masonry wall along Mason and Pine dates from before 1906, when it held up the hill beneath the Hopkins, and next door, the Stanford mansions. Leland Stanford (1824-93) was the founder of Stanford University.

10 Turn right on Powell Street. Just past Bush Street, on your right, is 535 Powell.

Political boss and gambler Frank Daroux bought this house for his wife, Tessie Wall, in 1912. Tessie ran the city's best early 20th-century brothel. Frank fell in love with Tessie when they were both about 40 – he loved her social prominence and "big tastes". On their first date, they drank 20 bottles of wine. At their wedding, 105 guests consumed a 150-pound wedding cake and 80 cases of champagne. But once they were married, Frank wanted her out of "the business". When she refused, he left her for another woman. Tessie's response: she shot him with a 22-calibre revolver. His injuries were minor but the divorce was final. As she explained to the police: "I shot him because I love him – damn him!"

11 Continue walking downhill on Powell to Union Square or catch the Powell Street cable car.

OPPOSITE: A GRAND HOUSE ON NOB HILL

FOUNTAIN OF THE TORTOISES IN HUNTINGTON PARK

WALK 11

Dead Sailors and Exuberant Artists

With a strong sense of neighbourhood, Russian Hill is a place of urban elegance as well as the haunt of off-beat artists and bohemians.

One cable car climbs past the crest, another sweeps by at the base. Streets here are apt to turn abruptly into gardens and stairways when they become too steep for vehicles. Cross-town traffic is diverted under the hill through a tunnel. Russian Hill is a stone's throw from North Beach and downtown but so hard to get to it forms an urban island. In the 19th century, literati and artists congregated here. In the 20th century, they staged musical theatre in private apartments. In 1906, the fires swept through not once, but twice (on Thursday heading west, on Friday heading east), yet there are pockets of pre-1906 structures (saved by topography and cantankerous residents who wouldn't let go). You'll find a forgotten graveyard, the site of the city's first legal hanging, malicious ghosts in a house and friendly ghosts in a bell tower, a haunted hotel, prankster artists and writers, and the house where Robert Louis Stevenson's widow held séances to talk to him. You'll also find the best brothel in town (in the 1930s), run by Sally Stanford – who later became mayor of Sausalito.

1 Take the Hyde Street cable car or No. 41 or 45 bus to the corner of Hyde Street and Union Street. Walk downhill on Hyde to Russell Street. Turn right to 29 Russell.

Jack Kerouac stayed here in 1952 with Neal and Carolyn Cassady and their children. In his attic studio, Kerouac wrote *On the Road*. In the shared rooms downstairs, he fell in love with Carolyn.

2 Backtrack up Hyde. Turn right on Union Street. Cross Leavenworth Street and go uphill one-half block. Turn left on Macondray Lane. Stay on Macondray when it becomes a path. Be careful crossing Jones Street. Continue on Macondray for another half block (to the wooden staircase), then backtrack to Jones.

Although legally a street, Macondray is too narrow and too steep for vehicles. It is the setting – as Barbary Lane – for Armistead Maupin's *Tales of the City* books of pot-smoking, free-love, quintessentially 1960s San Francisco.

3 Turn left uphill at Jones Street. At Vallejo Street, take either the stairs or ramp uphill. Follow to the end of the road. This is the Russian Hill summit.

It's also the site of the first legal execution in San Francisco: 32-year-old Spanish cook and gambler José Forner y Brugada was hanged in 1852 for killing José Rodriguez. Forner y Brugada claimed self-defence.

WHERE TO EAT

1 JONA'S ON HYDE,
1800 Hyde Street at Vallejo;
Tel: 1-415-775-2517.
A relaxed corner deli serving sandwiches, salads, coffee. $

2 SWENSEN'S ICE CREAM,
1999 Hyde Street;
Tel: 1-415-775-6818.
Old-time San Francisco ice cream. $

3 XOX TRUFFLES,
754 Columbus Avenue;
Tel: 1-415-421-4814.
Treat yourself to chocolate! $$

In the 1860s, David Jobson built an observatory here to spy ships coming into the bay and be the first to rush to the Merchants' Exchange and buy or sell futures for incoming merchandise. At weekends, for a small fee, anyone could climb to the top.

Notice the dark shingle-clad houses at 1013-1019, 1034 and 1036 Vallejo. Atypical for San Francisco architecture, they were built in the 1880s and 1890s as a leaning towards nature and away from Victorian flamboyance. Willis Polk (1867-1924) designed Nos. 1013-19. (For more on Polk, see Walk 15.)

4 Take the stairs through the park (a continuation of Vallejo) to Taylor Street. Cross Taylor to Ina Coolbrith Park. Stay near the top of the park, unless you want to climb even more.

OPPOSITE: THE "HILLINESS" OF RUSSIAN HILL SEPARATES IT FROM THE CITY AROUND

DISTANCE **2.2 miles (3.5km) – some steep hills and stairs**

ALLOW **3 hours**

START **Corner of Hyde and Union Street**

FINISH **Chestnut and Mason Street**

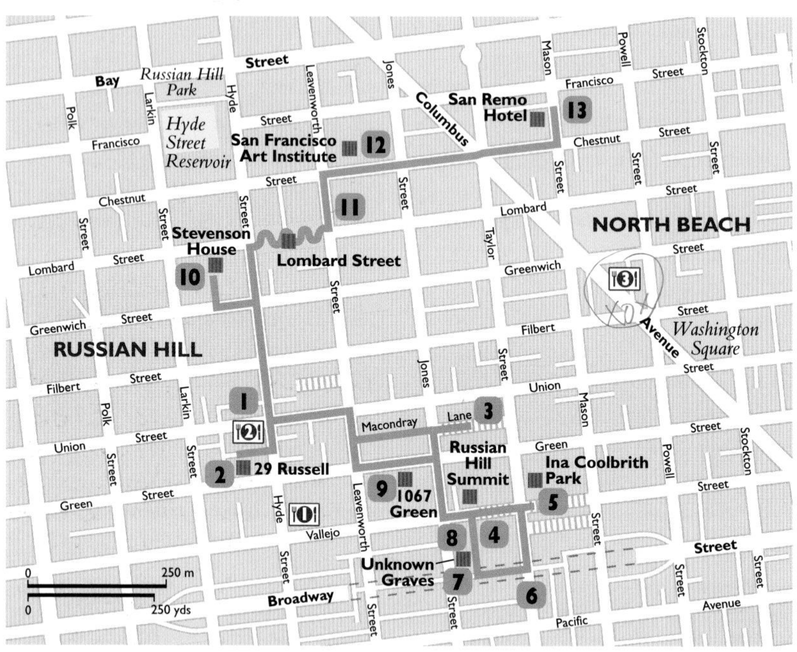

Ina Coolbrith (1841-1928) was a poet famed for her beauty, her poetry, and the literary salons that she hosted in the area. The house on your right, 1652-1656 Taylor, is the locally famous House of the Flag. In 1906, as fires approached, the owner was ordered to evacuate – he refused. Using water he'd saved in the bathtub and a soda siphon, he kept the flames at bay. Eventually, he fled, but first he raised a flag above his roof. Soldiers in the streets below were so moved, they raced up the hill and saved the house.

Behind you, across the street, at 1001 Vallejo, was the brothel run by Sally Stanford (1903-82). She later moved to Nob Hill (to a building since demolished), before retiring to Sausalito, where she was elected mayor at the age of 72.

5 With your back to Coolbrith Park, turn left down Taylor Street to Broadway.

Since 1952, a tunnel under Broadway Street has diverted east-west traffic, adding to local tranquillity. In an earlier – 1890s – attempt to tame the gradient and make these streets passable for vehicles, the city cut through the base of the hill, stranding the 1850s-era homes high above. The owners were forced to build the lengthy staircases and high retaining walls you see across the street. An unintended consequence was that the retaining walls served as a firebreak for the 1906 fires.

6 Cross Broadway and turn right uphill until the upper part of Broadway becomes a deadend. Cross to your right and climb the (unmarked) Florence Street staircase.

At the top of the stairs, pause to catch your breath but beware the spirits. Discovered and removed during the gold-rush era, this was once a graveyard where Russian crosses marked the 19th-century graves of unknown sailors or seal-hunters that were buried here.

7 Continue walking on Florence Street back to Vallejo.

At the corner on your left is the site where engineer-turned-comic writer Gelett Burgess (1866-1951) once lived. Perhaps it is here that he wrote his 1905 essay *The Ghost Extinguisher*, explaining techniques he developed using glass jars, formaldehyde and a bicycle pump to catch ghosts.

8 Turn left on Vallejo, then right down the ramp on Jones Street. At the corner, turn left on Green Street, and continue half way down the block.

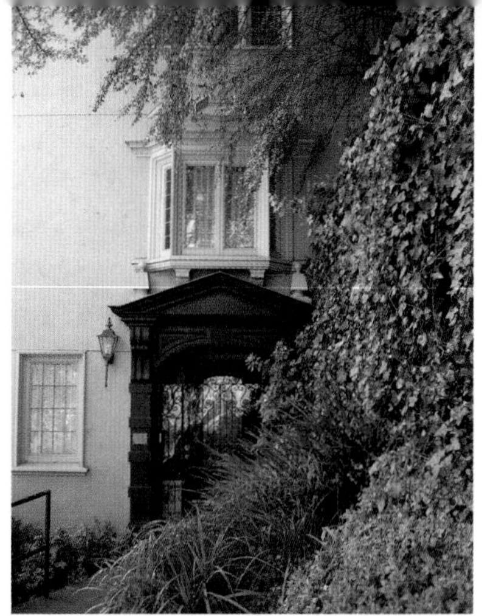

The Victorian houses on your left are 1906 survivors: most unusual is the Octagon House at 1067 Green, built in the 1850s to a design inspired by phrenologist, vegetarian and sex-educator Orson Fowler (1809-87). Fowler argued the octagon was ideal for creating sunlit spaces, promoting sanitary and healthful living, and improving occupants' sexual vigour.

By the way, Green Street was named for gold-rush era mayoral candidate Paul Geddes, aka Talbot H Green. While campaigning, Mr "Green" was recognized as defaulting bank clerk Geddes, who had left wife, children and debts behind in Philadelphia to come to California and make it rich.

9 Continue on Green Street. Turn right at Leavenworth, then left on Union and right on Hyde. At Greenwich Street, turn left up to George Sterling Park.

ABOVE: SALLY STANFORD'S BROTHEL, CONSIDERED THE BEST IN TOWN IN THE 1930s

STOP

Read the wall plaque for details on poet George Sterling (1869-1926) and six-times Wimbledon tennis champion Alice Marble (1913-90). Then walk to the far side of the tennis courts for a view of the Stevenson House, 1100 Lombard (across the street, on the righthand corner). After Robert Louis Stevenson (1850-94) died in Samoa, his widow, the former Fannie Osbourne returned to San Francisco and commissioned Willis Polk to design this house. Attempting to contact Robert's spirit, she held séances here, which were well attended, in part perhaps because of Fannie's legendary beauty and charm. Perhaps Robert had been listening because, in 1906, the rampaging fires did not damage the house.

10 Exit George Sterling Park and backtrack to Hyde Street. Turn left and walk down Lombard Street, known as the Crookedest Street in the city.

Until 1922, the 27% gradient here made the then-cobbled straight street difficult for cars and horse-drawn carriages to climb. Residents petitioned the city to build in some curves. At the bottom of the street, 1000 Lombard was Pat Montandon's home. As she explains in her book *Intruders* (published in 1975), one night she forgot to bring a drink to the tarot card reader entertaining at her party. The card reader cursed her, and the next year went bad. Montandon's dog growled at unseen chills, screams echoed through the house, friends committed suicide, and an unidentified body was found after a fire.

11 Turn left on Leavenworth, turn right on Chestnut and then left into the San Francisco Art Institute, 800 Chestnut.

Friendly ghosts are known to occupy the bell tower here. When it's time to close up for the night, after the guard has turned off all the lights, it's not uncommon for the lights to flicker back to life. (You can see a Diego Rivera mural here.)

SAN FRANCISCO ART INSTITUTE;
800 CHESTNUT STREET;
www.sfai.edu

12 Continue on Chestnut Street for two blocks, turn left on Mason and walk to the San Remo Hotel, on your left at 2237 Mason.

According to legend, when the "girls" and the "johns" checked out of this Prohibition-era speakeasy and brothel, the ghost of the madam stayed on, and sometimes knocks on the door of room 33. The spirit of a little girl has been seen here too, roaming the hallways and trying to get into room 42.

SAN REMO HOTEL;
2237 MASON STREET;
www.sanremohotel.com

13 When you're ready to return, backtrack on Chestnut to Columbus Avenue and catch the Mason Street cable car or the No. 20 or 30 bus.

OPPOSITE: LOMBARD STREET, JUSTIFIABLY KNOWN AS THE CROOKEDEST STREET IN THE CITY

WALK 12

Art and Scoundrels in the City's Civic Center

Civic Center – world-class symphony, ballet, opera and art – and City Hall – built on an old graveyard and the ruins of scandalous political shenanigans.

In April 1906, the ruins of the "New" City Hall were all the proof San Franciscans needed that the city was run by crooks. As they said, City Hall had been built with a "mix of bad politics and bad cement". But the phoenix was the official city bird, and a symbol of the city's spirit (never mind that the phoenix is a mythical creature not a bird, which is why the California quail became the city's official bird). We would rise from the ashes better than before. Rebuilding in the private sector started before the fires' heat had cooled. Public buildings took longer: resources were exhausted, tax revenue gone, and voters were disgusted. But as preparation for the 1915 Panama-Pacific International Exposition became reality, we wanted to prove that San Francisco was a great city, and building of the new current City Hall began. Funding for the great arts centres – museums, symphony hall and the opera house – would come later. Perhaps because Civic Center was not hastily built, it is today a beautiful gathering of grand buildings. This easy walk is best on weekdays when City Hall is open.

1 Take the underground Muni train to Civic Center station and exit by United Nations Plaza. Or take the historic F-line street car to Hyde or Leavenworth. Or walk down Market Street from Powell. The plaza is on the right.

"To save succeeding generations from the scourge of war, ... to reaffirm faith in fundamental human rights, ... to promote social progress and better standards of life in larger freedom." Between April and June 1945, delegates of 50 nations met in San Francisco to organize the new United Nations. Our place in the world is marked in the pavement with longitude and latitude.

2 At the end of the Plaza, cross Hyde Street, and pass the Founders' Statue (which had stood near here before 1906 and survived). Ahead is Civic Center Plaza, and beyond that, beaux-arts City Hall (more on City Hall shortly). Turn right on Larkin Street to the Asian Art Museum, 200 Larkin.

This is the site of the Yerba Buena Cemetery (1850-60). Shifting sands sometimes uncovered the shallow graves, marked only with flat boards; some caskets were filled with rocks, as grave diggers were paid by the grave not the body. In 1870, most remains were removed, but a few more were found during construction here in 2001. The cemetery became the site of the "New" City Hall, built with shoddy construction between 1871 and 1898, and destroyed in 1906.

The Asian Art Museum is a world-class collection of art from throughout Asia, and is now housed in what had been the main Public Library.

ASIAN ART MUSEUM;
200 LARKIN STREET; www.asianart.org

3 As you exit the museum, turn right on Larkin Street, cross McAllister Street and turn left. The building that fills this block is the State Supreme Court, at 350 McAllister.

San Francisco is not the state capital (that's Sacramento), but in the 1870s, the state Supreme Court established its home here. (The streets were less muddy, the liquor stronger, and the women more beautiful, or so it was claimed.) After passing through security, explore the art and civics exhibits in the lobby areas, and the panoramic painting of historic San Francisco downstairs.

OPPOSITE: THE INTERIOR OF CITY HALL; ABOVE: A BUDDHA ON DISPLAY AT THE ASIAN ART MUSEUM

DISTANCE 2.2 miles (3.5km)

ALLOW 2 hours

START United Nations Plaza, Market Street at Leavenworth

FINISH United Nations Plaza, Market Street at Leavenworth

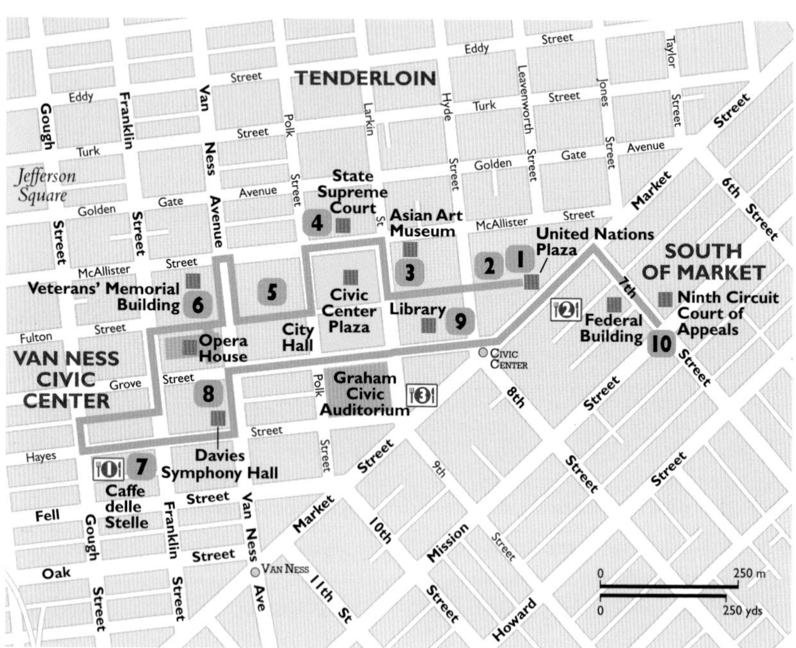

4 As you exit, continue walking right on McAllister Street, then left on Dr Carlton B Goodlett Place (Polk Street) and enter City Hall. (Note: City Hall is closed at weekends and on public holidays.)

City Hall was finished in 1915, just in time for the Panama-Pacific International Exposition. At 307ft 6in (94m), its dome is the fifth tallest in the world, and taller than the federal capitol in Washington DC by 42ft (13m).

It's common to see weddings in the rotunda: some 2,000 couples tie the knot here each year. In 1954, Marilyn Monroe married Joe DiMaggio here. As local columnist Art Hoppe explained, "The time and place of the wedding was kept a closely guarded secret and only about 500 people managed to hear about it in time to turn the corridors outside … into a madhouse." In 2004, around Valentine's Day, many same-sex marriages were performed here – the legality of those marriages then got hung up in the courts.

OPPOSITE: THE BEAUX-ARTS INTERIOR OF CITY HALL, WITH ITS IMPRESSIVE DOME

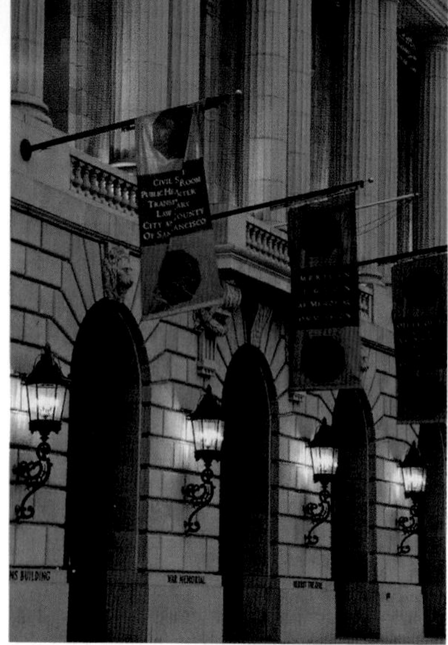

5 Leave City Hall on the opposite side from where you came in. You'll be on Van Ness Avenue, looking across at the War Memorial Opera House, and the Veterans' Memorial Building. To get there, turn right on Van Ness, cross at the corner and backtrack on the far side of Van Ness.

These two buildings, built in the 1930s, were meant to complement each other. The formal meetings and official signing of the United Nations Charter took place in them in 1945. On the right is the Veterans's Memorial Building, home to a performing arts library and museum, the Herbst Theatre, and many offices. Several organizations present programmes at Herbst, including San Francisco Performances (www.performances.org), and City Arts & Lectures (www.cityarts.net). On the left is the Opera House, home to the San Francisco Opera and the San Francisco Ballet.

By the way, you won't see ghosts here any more. Ghosts of old performers were known to lurk on stage after the audience had gone home, the lights were out and the house was dark but now, an empty stage always has a strong light left blazing – known as a ghost light – to scare away the ghosts.

6 Walk through the park that separates the Opera House and the Veterans' Memorial Building. At the far side, turn left on Franklin Street. Cross to the other side of Franklin at Grove and carry on. Turn right on Ivy Street. Turn left on Gough, then left on Hayes Street.

Look across at the Caffe delle Stelle, 395 Hayes, the site of the 1906 "Ham 'n' Eggs" Fire. At around 9am on 18 April 1906, several hours after the pre-dawn earthquake that started fires elsewhere, a mother in this still-safe district wanted to make a ham-and-eggs breakfast for the family. The wooden houses here had fared well in the quake but, unbeknown to her, the quake had damaged her chimney. The fire in her stove set her home alight. Soon, this fire destroyed not only her home, but the whole neighbourhood, before sweeping on through and wiping out what the earthquake hadn't already destroyed of City Hall.

7 Continue on Hayes Street. At Van Ness Avenue, turn left and walk along the side of Davies Symphony Hall, home to the San Francisco Symphony. Stop at the sculpture, at the corner of Grove and Van Ness.

ABOVE: THE ELEGANT EXTERIOR OF THE VETERANS' MEMORIAL BUILDING, BUILT IN 1932

From the 1870s (when construction on City Hall started nearby) until 1906, St Ignatius Convent and College filled this entire block. The morning of the earthquake, crowds flocked to confess and hear mass in the still largely unharmed chapel – but the Ham 'n' Eggs fire soon reduced it all to ashes. (St Ignatius would later become the University of San Francisco.)

When the symphony hall first opened, the acoustics were less than optimal but a number of adjustments were made and now it works – it can even be "tuned" to accommodate both small and large orchestras, and even chamber concerts.

8 Cross Van Ness Avenue. Turn right on Grove Street. As you pass Civic Center Plaza again, the building ahead of you is the main branch of the San Francisco Public Library, 100 Larkin Street. Continue alongside and enter the Grove Street entrance.

Notice the displays just inside the entrance: household goods and other objects found during excavation. Rotating exhibits outside the San Francisco History Center on the sixth floor are excellent.

9 As you exit the library, continue on Grove Street until it ends at Market Street. Turn left on Market to 7th Street. Cross 7th Street and turn right. (This is a rundown area but it's only a short walk.) The huge building on the right is the new Federal Building (not open to the public). Across the street, on the left, is the Ninth Circuit Court of Appeals.

Now the most controversial court in the nation, the building started as a post office and court house in the 1890s. Quirks in funding allowed a budget to pay to import Italian artisans to decorate corridors and ceilings in mosaics. Guided tours on Tuesday, every other week.

10 Backtrack on 7th Street to Market. Catch the F-line street car (going right towards downtown), or walk right on Market to the cable car line or underground street cars at Powell.

WHERE TO EAT

1 CAFFE DELLE STELLE,
395 Hayes Street;
Tel: 1-415-252-1110.
Italian fare with French waiters – popular among symphony, opera and ballet goers for pre-performance meals. $$

2 CAFFE TRINITY,
1145 Market Street;
Tel: 1-415-864-3333.
Small cafe with great atmosphere, serving coffee and snacks. $

3 ANANDA-FUARA VEGETARIAN,
1298 Market Street at Larkin;
Tel: 1-415-621-1994.
Hearty and inexpensive meals in a spiritual, friendly atmosphere. $

CITY HALL IN ALL ITS GLORY

WALK 13

The Famous Houses of Postcard Row

Learn about the houses of Postcard Row at Alamo Square, and cross paths with a murderous squatter, a few gangsters and Guglielmo Marconi.

San Franciscans love Victorian houses now but that wasn't always the case. In the late 19th century, some elegant mansions were constructed but most contemporary housing was of no particular consequence, built of then-abundant local redwood dressed up to look like Italian marble. As decades passed and styles changed, some Victorian houses were made over in the latest fashion; some lost a fanciful façade to a drab layer of low-maintenance plaster or aluminium siding. In the 1950s, the housing policy was "out with the old, in with the new", and a 27-block area between Alamo Square and Japantown was demolished in a redevelopment programme. In the 1960s, the policy changed to "we're losing our heritage – somebody save the Victorians!" And save we did. This walk skirts the edge of the redevelopment zone, lets you peek at marvellous Victorians, and gives you enough insider knowledge to appreciate the Victorian buildings that you see anywhere in San Francisco.

1 **Take the No. 22 Fillmore bus to Haight Street and Fillmore. Walk East on Haight Street. Turn right on Buchanan Street to 201 Buchanan, the Nightingale House.**

Built in 1883 for gold-rush immigrant, politico and real-estate developer John Nightingale and his family, this house doesn't look like its neighbours, nor is it attached to them. Even if we didn't know from other sources that Mr Nightingale was financially comfortable, the house's architecture would give us the clues we need. The scale is modest yet the design is unique (you'll see elements but not the whole in other houses).

2 **Backtrack up Buchanan to Haight Street and turn right and continue on Haight to Laguna Street.**

198 Haight was built in 1884 for real-estate speculator and self-proclaimed "capitalist" Thomas Welch McMorey. Unlike most San Francisco houses, it stayed in the McMorey family for a century. The house's details are typically Italianate, a style much in vogue in the 1870s and 1880s. With the pretension that San Francisco had much in common with European tradition, houses were built from locally available redwood but made to look like stone. To identify an Italianate, look for a sense of height, a flat roofline, slanted bay windows and classical columns.

3 **Turn left on Laguna to Page Street. Notice 294 Page.**

This house was built in the late 1880s when the Stick style (featuring flat board banding and other ornamentation applied in geometric patterns, hence "stick") replaced the earlier fondness for Italianate.

As wood-shaping technology became more mechanized, builders started to experiment. Like an Italianate, a Stick house has a tall, flat roofline, but the easiest way to distinguish the two is by the shape of their bay windows – the Stick has square bays. In addition, like the Nightingale House (see Step 1 above), 294 Page is larger and more embellished than its neighbours – a good clue that it was designed by an architect rather than a builder (who would have stuck to standard designs).

4 **Turn left on Page Street.**

OPPOSITE: PICTURESQUE POSTCARD ROW; ABOVE: ORNATE ARCHITECTURAL DETAIL

DISTANCE 2 miles (3.2km) – some hills

ALLOW 2 hours

START Haight Street at Fillmore

FINISH Fillmore Street

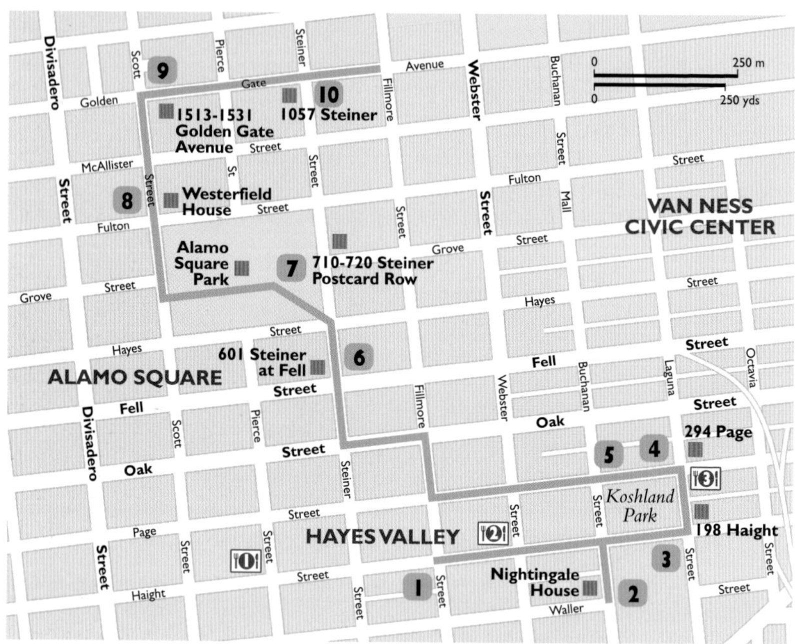

As you walk along, notice Italianate houses as well as Sticks. You'll also start to see another style of Victorian – one that shows off the angles of the gabled roof. Instead of hiding the roof behind a high, flat false front like its earlier cousins, this style – dubbed "Queen Anne" – dropped the pretensions of the Old World masonry palazzo, and became a showcase for all the imaginative things that can be done with wood; see, for example, 584 Page. You'll come across several more Queen Anne houses very soon.

5 Continue on Page Street. At Fillmore, turn right (uphill). Turn left on Oak. Turn right on Steiner to the corner of Fell Street.

Notice 601 Steiner at Fell. This house is a fun example of Queen Anne style, and it comes with lots of stories, none of them confirmed. Masonry contractor James Scobie, for whom it was built in 1893, lived here for less than two years. After Scobie moved on, it is rumoured to have been an elegant house of assignation, which deteriorated over the years into a less exclusive brothel. In the 1920s, it was a sanitorium, and also thought to shelter gangsters from out of state (this was the period of Prohibition, when Chicago's Al Capone and others flourished). By the 1940s, it was a run-down rooming house, and more recently transformed into a drug- and alcohol-rehabilitation centre.

6 Continue on Steiner Street to Alamo Square Park. Enter the park, and look back at 710-720 Steiner – the famous Postcard Row.

Any Victorian house commands a premium in today's real-estate market, but in their day most were built for those of modest means. This row of six shows the common practice among contractors who drew on economies of scale by building nearly identical houses side-by-side. Here, builder Matthew Kavanaugh gave all these 1894 Queen Annes the same floor plan. For individuality he varied window placement and other decorative elements. He did this for a sale price of $3,500 each – less than half the price of 294 Page Street. (By the way, these houses don't have big round towers like you saw at 601 Steiner, but the fact that the gabled roof isn't hidden is your clue that these are Queen Annes.)

If your feet get wet crossing Alamo Square, consider yourself part of history. The park was named for the poplar tree (*alamo* in Spanish) that grew by the fresh water spring here. In the Spanish period, riders travelling between the Presidio and the Mission knew to look for this tree, which signalled an ideal resting spot. In the years before 1868, Alamo Square provided shelter for Dutch Charlie Duane, a violent, sometimes murderous and tenacious squatter. In 1906, Alamo Square became a refugee camp. In the 20th century, the young violinist Yehudi Menuhin (1916-99) came with his sister from their nearby home and played on the same lawn you are walking on.

WHERE TO EAT

1 BURGER JOINT,
700 Haight Street at Pierce;
Tel: 1-415-864-3833.
www.burgerjointsf.com
This popular place serves, reputedly, the best hamburgers to be found anywhere in the US. $

2 ROTEE,
400 Haight Street at Webster;
Tel: 1-415-552-8309.
www.roteesf.com
Affordable Indian and Pakistani cuisine in a fun Bollywood atmosphere. $$

3 SIDEWALK CAFÉ,
297 Page Street at Laguna;
Tel: 1-415-863-7373.
Like it says, a neighbourhood cafe with sidewalk seating. $

7 Walk uphill through the park. As you approach Scott Street, you can't help but notice the Stick-style Westerfeld House (with square bays), 1198 Fulton Street at Scott.

Despite the fanciful gossip, this palazzo was never a Russian Embassy, nor was it home to Charles Manson (see Walk 18). In reality, it was designed by architect Henry Geilfuss in 1889 for commercial baker and candy-maker William Westerfeld. In 1906, Westerfeld's widow and son sold to John J Mahoney (the contractor responsible for revamping the St Francis and Palace hotels). His friend Guglielmo Marconi may have used the tower for early radio transmissions.

By the 1930s, White Russians used the house as their community centre, and the basement became the Dark Eyes restaurant. At some point after the Russians moved out, a magician lived in the tower room and kept 500 candles burning continuously. During the Hippie era, famous residents included underground filmmaker Kenneth Anger, and Ken Kesey and his Calliope Company commune. In *The Electric Kool-Aid Acid Test*, author Thomas Wolfe immortalized it as "a freaking decayed giant known as the Russian Embassy".

8 Continue on Scott, walking downhill to Golden Gate Avenue. Turn right. Look at the bank of houses, 1513-1531 Golden Gate Avenue.

This wonderful row was built in 1875 by a contracting company called The Real Estate Associates (TREA), who built several thousand houses in San Francisco before going bankrupt. (Their financial woes may have been rooted in an overly aggressive programme of loans to potential buyers.) The style is Italianate, with a flat

roofline and angled bay windows. Catch any of these from the side, and you see the false front designed to give an illusion of height and majesty.

9 Continue on Golden Gate Avenue to Steiner Street and look at the corner house, 1057 Steiner.

Once called the Chateau Tivoli, this 1890 Queen Anne now shines in all her glory: with towers, rounded bay windows, arches and 22 rooms. Oregon lumber baron Daniel B Jackson may have had it designed for himself, or perhaps it was a boarding house from the start. For a time, it was the private residence of the owner of San Francisco's Tivoli Opera House. In the 1930s, a Yiddish school and cultural centre found a home here; by the 1960s, it provided shelter for a commune and various New Age groups.

10 To pick up the No. 22 Fillmore bus again, continue one block to Fillmore.

OPPOSITE: TYPICAL QUEEN ANNE HOUSE; ABOVE: THE CONTRASTING STYLE OF A TREA ITALIANATE HOUSE

WALK 14

Sushi and Sayonara in Japantown

Japantown is a vibrant district with layers of history, culture and religion. Its lovely present-day atmosphere does much to hide its rather dark past.

The Japanese who moved here after 1906, when previous owner-residents scattered, were banned from owning property but created a comfortable community for themselves, with their own grocery stores and restaurants. Then in 1942, with war declared, the US President issued an order that everyone of Japanese heritage was to leave coastal areas near military bases. Practically overnight, thousands of Japanese and Japanese-American residents and business owners packed up a suitcase or two and got on trains to internment camps. Four years later, when the war was over, former residents returned and found what they'd had now belonged to others. Many moved away; others settled in and started again. Soon, post-war aesthetics spurred yet another displacement: as part of a massive "redevelopment" project, 27 blocks of old buildings in Japantown and to the south across Geary Street were razed. New housing projects were constructed nearby and a brand new Japantown was created.

1 Take the No. 38 bus to Laguna, Buchanan or Webster Streets. (Nos. 2, 3 or 4 on Sutter also get you here.) Walk to the Peace Plaza, at Post and Buchanan. Enter the Peace Plaza from Post Street at Buchanan.

This is a quiet place to sit, unless there's a festival, in which case you're likely to hear and see some exuberant taiko drumming. The stylized modern Peace Pagoda was a gift from Japan.

2 With your back to the Pagoda and facing Post Street, enter the doors on your left, to the Kintetsu Mall.

This mall was designed to feel like a rural town at night. Stroll through, shop for a kimono or teaset if you like, then continue walking. Heading straight, the pathway rises then falls again and soon you'll get to the enormous Kinokuniya bookstore (with books and magazines in both English and Japanese). Backtrack and turn right into the area meant to feel like a rural town in spring time. If you can tear your eyes away from the delicious-looking food, be sure to check out the flower arrangements in the Ikenobo Ikebana Society windows.

3 Leave the mall where you entered, cross to your left through the Peace Plaza, and cross Post Street to reach the Buchanan Street outdoor pedestrian mall.

At the corner, on your right, is Soko Hardware, 1698 Post, a hardware and variety store with a wonderful assortment of kitchenware downstairs. Soko is the local Japanese term for SF, or San Francisco.

Next door to Soko Hardware is the small but friendly National Japanese American Historical Society, 1684 Post, which is well worth a quick visit.

Back on Buchanan Street, the cobblestones, sculptures and fountains are designed to create the aura of a stylized streambed and origami figures.

OPPOSITE: A FEAST FOR THE EYES AT KINTETSU MALL; ABOVE: IKENOBO IKEBANA WINDOW DISPLAYS

DISTANCE **1.5 miles (2.4km) – some hills**

ALLOW **1.5 hours**

START **The Peace Plaza, at Post and Buchanan**

FINISH **Octavia and Sutter**

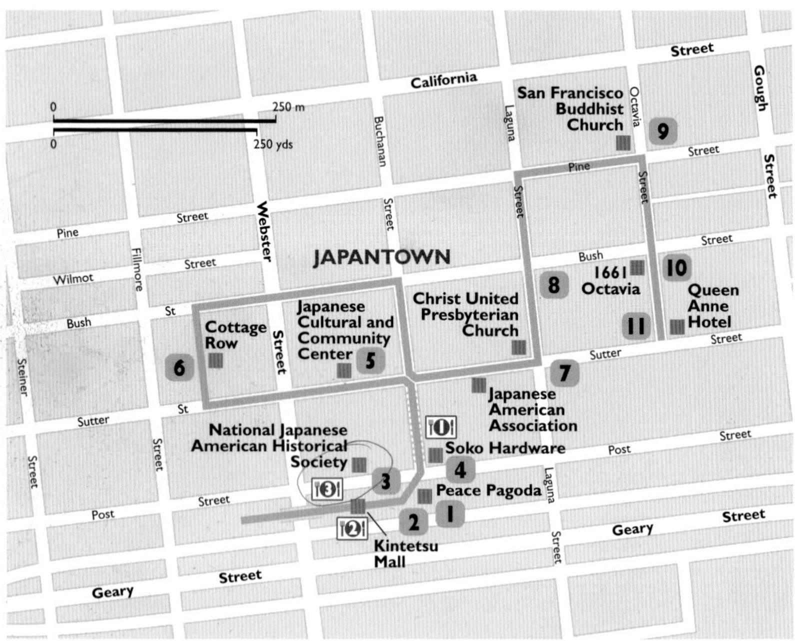

The sculptor was Japanese-American Ruth Asawa, whose work can also be seen at Ghirardelli Square (Walk 20), and in the tower of the de Young Museum (Walk 19). When Ruth was 16, she and her family were sent to the internment camps. Recently, reflecting on the experience, she graciously said: "I hold no hostilities for what happened; I blame no one. Sometimes good comes through adversity. I would not be who I am today had it not been for the Internment, and I like who I am."

4 Turn left and continue on Buchanan. Cross Sutter Street and turn left.

Here is the Japanese Cultural and Community Center of Northern California, an important meeting place housed in a modern building designed to look like old Japan.

JAPANESE CULTURAL AND COMMUNITY CENTER OF NORTHERN CALIFORNIA;
1840 SUTTER STREET;
www.jcccnc.org

OPPOSITE: A SCULPTURE IN THE PEACE PLAZA REMEMBERING JAPANESE-AMERICANS SENT TO WARTIME CAMPS

I AM
AN
MERICAN
JAPANES
ANCESTRY

5 Continue on Sutter to the middle of the next block. Turn right up the steps into the Cottage Row historic district.

All of a sudden, it feels like you've left Japantown – but this is just one of the layers of the district. This series of houses with shared walls – and other Victorian houses you see as you walk along – date from the late 19th century, an era when local merchants and professionals commuted on the Sutter Street cable car to work in the downtown retail or financial districts. Cottage Row was home to servants, while the larger houses on major thoroughfares were for those of more substantial means.

6 Continue on through Cottage Row. As you leave, turn right on Bush Street. Pass the Kinmon Gakuen language school, 2031 Bush. Turn right on Buchanan. Turn left on Sutter. As you continue on Sutter Street, you pass in front of Hokka Nichi Bei Kai, home of the Japanese American Association of Northern California. Continue on Sutter to the corner of Laguna.

The two religious institutions on the corners here demonstrate the spiritual wealth of this community. On your left is the Christ United Presbyterian Church, 1700 Sutter, which doesn't represent traditional Japanese religion, but rather the Western-orientation of many Japanese emigrants. Across the street on the right is the Sokoji (Zen) Temple, at 1691 Laguna. This Soto Zen Buddhist temple founded in 1934 (and moved to this new building in 1984) attracts many San Franciscans followers who are not of Japanese heritage.

JAPANESE AMERICAN ASSOCIATION OF NORTHERN CALIFORNIA;
1759 SUTTER STREET; www.nichibeikai.org

7 Turn left on Laguna. At Bush Street, cross and look back. Here, cultural overlays and blending reappear in a different guise.

On your right is the Konko Church, at 1909 Bush, a Shinto temple built in 1973. You are welcome to visit the rather simple front garden, and to go inside the temple. Be sure to remove your shoes before entering!

Across the street, 1881 Bush is now home to Kokoro, an assisted living facility for ageing Japanese-Americans. The somewhat peculiar façade is explained when you know that this building originally served as a synagogue in the late 19th and early 20th centuries, when the area was home to many Jewish professionals.

8 Continue up Laguna. Turn right on Pine Street and continue to the corner of Octavia Street.

The rather plain big building across the street is the San Francisco Buddhist Church, 1881 Pine. It is the oldest congregation of the Buddhist Churches of America, and inside the plain exterior is a stupa with ashes of the Buddha, a gift from the Emperor of Siam (Thailand).

9 Turn right (downhill) on Octavia to the corner of Bush Street.

Here we peel back the layers of history, to the time before Japantown. An eye clinic now occupies the corner house at 1661 Octavia that was once the home of Thomas Bell, his wife, his son, and the head servant who wasn't really a servant at all. Wealthy Thomas Bell died in 1892 under suspicious circumstances. Malicious neighbours spoke of black magic, and fingers were pointed at Mary Ellen "Mammy" Pleasant, the head servant. However, it is unlikely that Mary Ellen was guilty of anything but being an intelligent, business-savvy, strong-willed free black woman. (Mythmakers like to make her a runaway slave but she was probably free-born, although she could have been active in the "underground railroad" that helped slaves escape to Canada and the northern US.) The pavement plaque amidst the eucalyptus trees commemorates Mary Ellen.

10 Continue walking along Octavia to Sutter Street.

On your left is the Queen Anne Hotel, 1590 Sutter, built in 1890 as Miss Mary Lake's School for Girls, and closed in about 1896. It then served (until 1912) as the social and residential Cosmos Gentleman's Club. In 1900 – before there was a Japantown here or anywhere else in San Francisco – eight Japanese men worked as waiters and kitchen staff at Cosmos. In the 1920s and 1930s, it housed the Episcopal Dioceses' Girls Friendly Society Lodge, then remained vacant for decades before a complete renovation and relaunch in the 1990s as a hotel. But, through all the building's incarnations, it is said that one of Miss Mary's most diligent teachers was unhappy when the school closed, and vowed to stay on forever. Guests in her former room (No. 410) sometimes wake to see her sitting peacefully on the edge of the bed.

WHERE TO EAT

1 SHABUSEN,
1726 Buchanan Street;
Tel: 1-415-440-0466.
They call it Japanese fondue – cook your food by "swish-swishing" it in hot broth. $$

2 ISOBUNE SUSHI,
in the Kintetsu Mall on Post Street;
Tel: 1-415-563-1030.
Choose delicacies that float by on the conveyor belt; pay by the number of dishes you accumulate. $$

3 NIJIYA MARKET,
1737 Post Street (SE corner Webster);
Tel: 1-415-563-1901.
Buy exotic snacks here. $

11 Backtrack on Sutter to Laguna. Catch the No. 2, 3 or 4 Muni bus here. To catch the No. 38 bus back downtown, backtrack on Sutter, turn left on Laguna, and catch the bus on the other side of Geary.

THE MODERN, STYLIZED PEACE PAGODA IN THE PEACE PLAZA, A GIFT TO THE CITY FROM JAPAN

WALK 15

The Rich and Infamous of Pacific Heights

Gaze in awe at the mansions of Pacific Heights and their views across the Bay. Giggle in shock at scandalous histories of notorious residents.

This walk takes you through gorgeous Pacific Heights, with spectacular views and some hills. The area has been home to consulates and embassies, corporate titans, Hollywood stars and directors, best-selling authors, top physicians, politicians, eccentrics, madams and not a few ghosts. Pacific Heights became an increasingly fashionable neighbourhood for the well heeled after Nob Hill filled up in the late 1800s, and especially after Nob Hill burned in 1906. The houses here are big. More than one mansion was large enough to become a school when the family could no longer afford to maintain it. Some single-family homes have been converted to apartment blocks. The houses are beautiful and there are some grand Victorian ones, but because residents could afford the best architects, many of whom wanted to contradict the excesses and flamboyance of Victorian style, you will also see neo-classical designs. Willis Polk was a favourite architect in Pacific Heights. He has been characterized as an *enfant terrible,* argumentative, cantankerous but also brilliant and imaginative – you be the judge.

1 Take the No. 1 bus to California and Pierce Street, walk uphill on Pierce into Alta Plaza Park. (Notice the scars that were left when a Volkswagen flew down these stairs in the film *What's up, Doc?*.) Cross to the other side of the park, to Jackson Street.

Ahead, 2622 Jackson (with the mottled green tiled roof), was designed by young Willis Polk. In 1941, it was the Japanese consular residence; the day before the Pearl Harbor attack, the blaze in the chimney (destroying secret documents) was such that neighbours alerted the fire department. In 1950, this was a music school, and is now the home of a Hollywood filmmaker.

To the right, the French flag marks 2570 Jackson, a sometime residence of the French Consul General. The tall building beyond is luxury co-op apartments. Hillary Clinton, Bill Clinton, Al Gore, Barack Obama and Nancy Pelosi are all friendly with the penthouse residents.

2 Turn left on Jackson, then right at Divisadero Street to Pacific Avenue. Nearing the crest, the masonry structures on your right are the Ellinwood house (more on this later). Turn left and stroll three blocks along Pacific.

In the first block, pass 2820 Pacific Avenue on the right. Here, Willis Polk used a narrow lot stretching to Broadway for a home with a view for social activist Alice Griffith and her sister Carolyn in 1910. (You'll see the front of the house from Broadway soon.) At the next corner, 2889 Pacific was the Folger (coffee company) family home.

In the second block, pass 2900 Pacific, the Irish consulate in 1945, and 2961 Pacific, originally a single-family home, later converted to a group home for the Delancy Street Foundation, an against-all-odds self-help organization.

At the corner, look left to 2233 and 2255 Lyon, both Willis Polk designs.

3 Turn right on Lyon Street and right again on Broadway Street. Stay on the lefthand side.

Several houses here were built to enjoy views of the 1915 Panama-Pacific International Exposition; 2970 Broadway was built for Sidney and Florence Ehrman, music lovers and patrons of young violinist Yehudi Menuhin (1916-99), who practised here.

There's another Willis Polk at 2960 Broadway (and more at 2880, 2840, 2808 and 2800 Broadway).

Uphill at the corner is 2901 Broadway, the most expensive house in the city, offered for sale in 2006 for $55 million. Across the street to the left is 2898 Broadway, the former residence of attorney Melvin "King of Torts" Belli, and his wife Lia. During their stormy 1988 divorce, Belli called Lia "El Trampo" and accused her of throwing their pet dog off the Golden Gate Bridge. He was ultimately compelled to pay her $15 million in alimony. Lia later married a Romanian prince.

OPPOSITE: ALTA PLAZA PARK, PACIFIC HEIGHTS

DISTANCE 2.5 miles (4km) – expect hills

ALLOW 3-4 hours

START California and Pierce Street

FINISH Sacramento Street

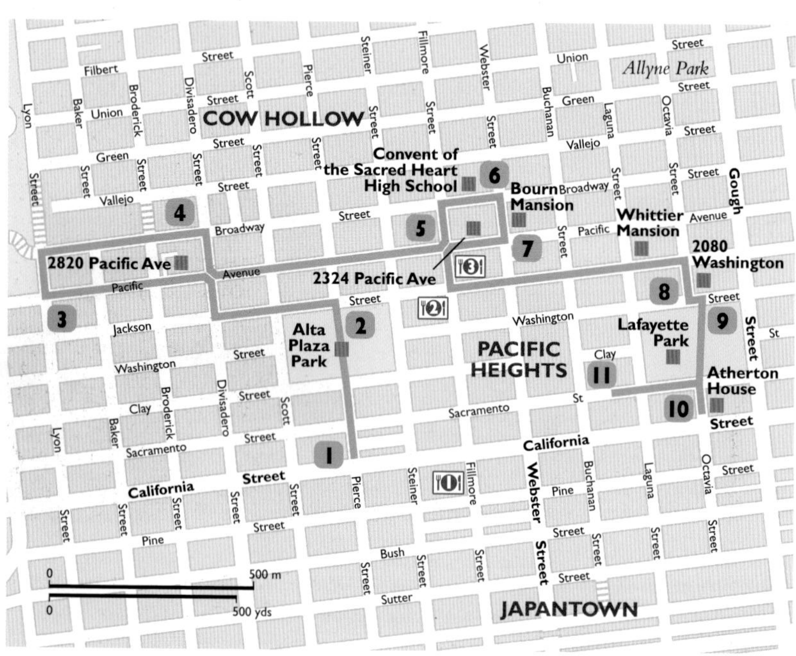

Charles Howard, who was the owner of champion racehorse Seabiscuit, lived at 2801 Broadway (at the corner). In the next block is the front of the narrow house that Polk designed for the Griffith sisters (the back of the house was visible on Pacific).

4 Turn right on Divisadero Street, then left on Pacific Avenue.

At 2799 Pacific is the Ellinwood mansion again, built in the 1890s for the highly regarded Welsh physician Charles Ellinwood (1834-1917). Scandal hit after the death of his friend, Dr Levy Lane, founder of Cooper (later Stanford) Medical College. Lane's estate was divided between the college and Ellinwood, with the intention that Ellinwood pass his part back to the college. Much to his colleagues' fury, Ellinwood kept the bequest for himself (but lost his job as president).

In 1945, the British Consul General lived at 2606 Pacific. More recently, 2516

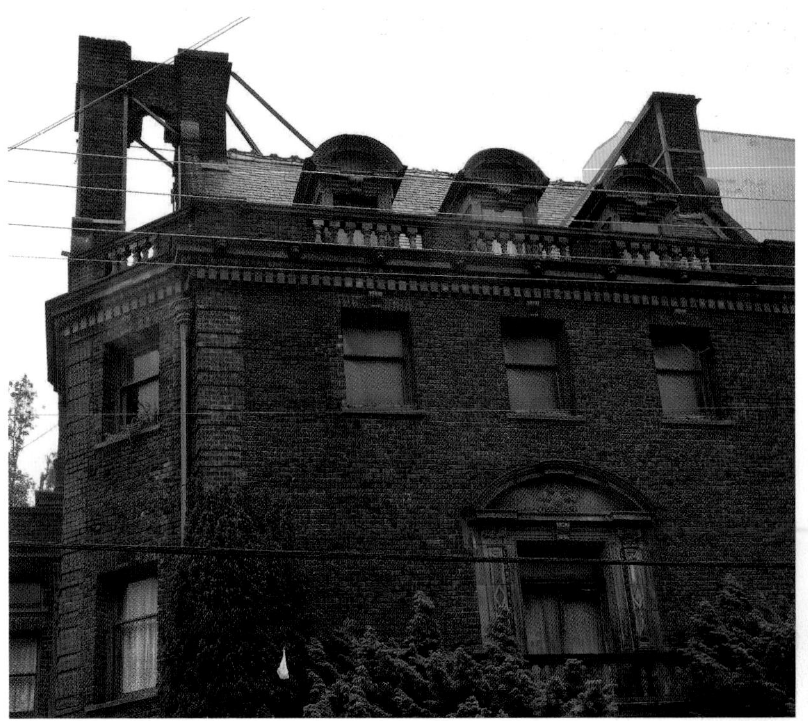

Pacific was the Consul's residence but Prime Minister Tony Blair thought it an unnecessary expense and forced the sale.

5 Turn left on Fillmore Street, then right on Broadway Street to 2222 Broadway, Convent of the Sacred Heart High School.

Having lost their Nob Hill home to fire in 1906, James L Flood, the bartender who made a fortune investing in Nevada silver mines, built this "house of marble on a hill of granite" for his wife Maud. After James died, Maud tried to give it to their beloved Episcopal Church but maintenance was too expensive and the church said no. Then, travelling incognito, in a curtained carriage, Maud secretly and successfully arranged a bequest to the Catholics instead.

6 Turn right on Webster Street, past the Italian consulate, to 2550 Webster, Bourn Mansion.

This early Willis Polk design for William Bourn, controversial president of Spring Valley Water Company (monopoly water supplier, 1865-1930) is wreathed in rumour. Some claim that acid parties were held and porno flicks filmed inside the dark "clinker" brick home, some even believe it to be haunted.

ABOVE: IMPOSING BOURN MANSION, ONE OF WILLIS POLK'S EARLY DESIGNS

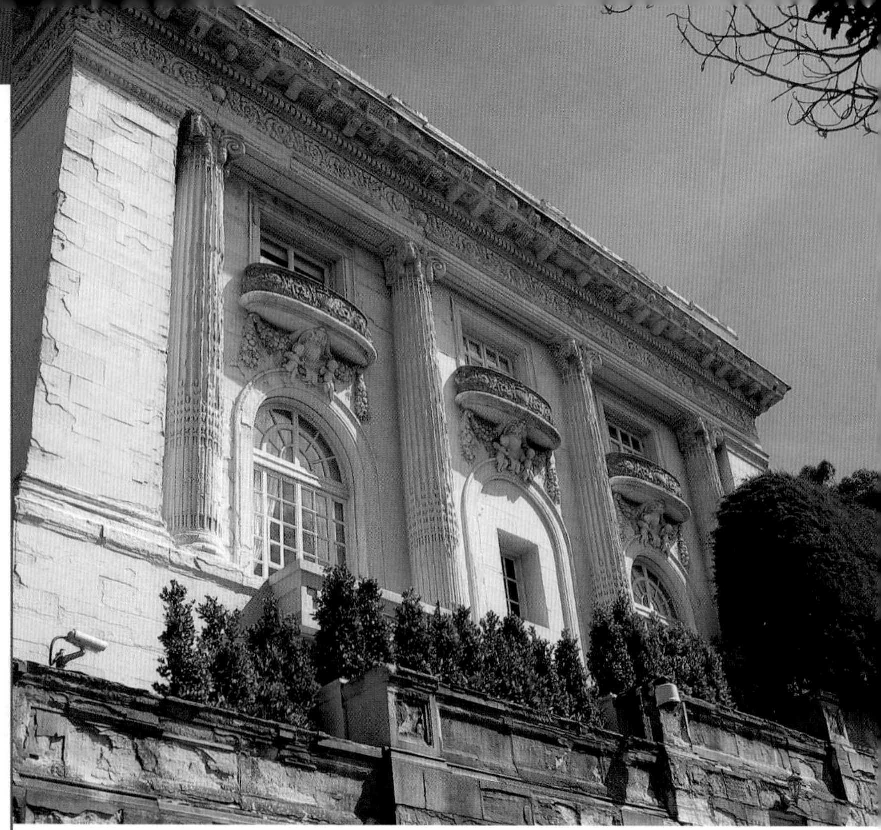

7 Turn right on Pacific Avenue. Pass by 2324 Pacific, former residence of San Francisco madam (later mayor of Sausalito) Sally Stanford (1903-82). Turn left on Fillmore, then left on Jackson.

2209 Jackson, which was built in 1870, is the last of what had been affordable houses on this block (named Tuckerville for the developer).

At the corner of Laguna Street is 2090 Jackson, the haunted Whittier Mansion built in 1896. The ghost (who enjoys the wine cellar) is either the original owner, paint manufacturer William Frank Whittier (1842-1917), or, more likely, his layabout son Billy. For a few months in 1941, this was the residence of handsome Fritz Wiedemann, the Nazi Consul to the US. He's said to have hidden secret papers behind an attic wall before he was evicted.

8 Continue on Jackson Street. Turn right up the curvy block of Octavia Street. On the left is 2080 Washington.

Sugar fortune heir Adolph Spreckels (1857-1924) built this mansion for his young wife, former artist's model Alma de Bretteville, in time for a bout of lavish entertaining during the 1915 Panama-

ABOVE: THE WHITE LIMESTONE SPRECKELS MANSION ON WASHINGTON STREET

Pacific International Exposition. Author Danielle Steel lived here in recent years.

Across the street, Lafayette Park was a 1906 refugee camp. In the 1800s, former City Attorney Samuel Holladay "squatted" here and built a home, arguing that parks were limited to a one-square block. He battled in court for 20 years after the city tried to oust him. (Holladay won.)

9 **Enter Lafayette Park at Octavia, and continue across. At the other side of the park, cross Sacramento Street. Walk downhill on Octavia to 1990 California, the Atherton House.**

When author Gertrude Atherton's (1857-1948) husband died at sea, his body was shipped home (without prior notice) pickled in a barrel of rum.

10 **Backtrack uphill on Octavia to Sacramento and turn left.**

2151 Sacramento, the medical offices in 1923 of Dr Albert Abrams, a brilliant diagnostician, experimenter with x-rays, professor at Cooper Medical College, and fraudulent claimant to a medical degree from Heidelberg. Abrams invented (and leased on franchise) the Dynomizer, Oscilloclast and Radioclast for diagnosing and treating cancer, diabetes, syphilis and other diseases with radio signals and by telephone. When the American Medical Association disputed his claims, among his defenders was Sir Arthur Conan Doyle, who may have visited during his lecture tour on spiritualism. (For more on spiritualism, visit the Golden Gate Spiritualist Church.)

At 2220 Sacramento, the Chambers Mansion was built in 1887 for silver miner and politician Robert Chambers. After Robert's death, Misses Alice, Margaret and Sarah Chambers lived here but ghost hunters claim it is the Chambers' heir Claudia (who was brutally murdered in the house) who haunts it. (It's now a private residence.)

GOLDEN GATE SPIRITUALIST CHURCH;

1901 FRANKLIN STREET; www.ggsc.org

11 **Catch the No. 1 Muni bus, which runs back to downtown along Sacramento Street.**

WHERE TO EAT

1 TULLY'S COFFEE,
2445 Fillmore Street;
Tel: 1-415-929-8808.
Friendly cafe, and a fine place to sit and relax. $

2 CHOUQUET'S,
2500 Washington Street at Fillmore;
Tel: 1-415-359-0075.
A relaxing place with a varied menu, for both lunch and dinner. $$

3 TANGO GELATO,
2015 Fillmore Street;
Tel: 1-415-346-3692.
Off the path but if you haven't been distracted by other Fillmore Street venues, try the gelato here. $$

WALK 16

Mission District – Birthplace of the City

Tread on Native American, Spanish and gold-rush era graves, skirt the flames of 1906 and, with a murderous aside, explore a lively modern area.

It's no coincidence that the place of longest continuous settlement – today's Mission district – has the best weather in the city. Native Americans avoided the foggy, wind-swept sand dunes in favour of the sunny warmth and creek-fed lagoons here – perfect for hunting and fishing. When Spanish missionaries arrived, they intended to convert the Indians and teach them to farm and ranch, so they chose a location with fresh water and good weather that Indians frequented. After Mexico won independence from Spain, and the Roman Catholic Church lost much of its power, mission holdings were reduced from vast estates to just the chapel and cemetery. Newcomers used tiles and bricks from old mission warehouses in other structures. Some buildings were converted to taverns and gambling establishments. In the gold-rush era, the plank-covered toll road through miles of sand dunes made this a weekend getaway spot for those living downtown. Later, as the city's population grew, dunes were tamed, roads were paved and trolley lines opened, and San Franciscans of all stripes came to live here.

1 **Take the J-Church street car to 20th and Church. Start at the top of Dolores Park (the south-west corner), at 20th Street and Church Street.**

Before you get swept away by the view, look across the trolley tracks just up Church Street to the golden fire hydrant. The Fire Chief comes here every year on 18 April, the anniversary of the 1906 earthquake and fire, and with some ceremony, repaints the hydrant gold. The fire never reached this point, and as one of the hydrants that never ran out of water (despite more than 300 water main breaks), it is a symbol of pride.

Turning to the downtown view, think back to when this was the edge of town. In the 19th century, Jewish cemeteries filled what is now the park. After they closed, the bodies were moved to Colma (the city south of San Francisco that boasts more dead than living inhabitants). In 1905, the City purchased the property, intending to use it as a park, but before it could be developed, the muddy mess became an impromptu refugee camp for those burned out in 1906.

Now local city-dwellers consider the park a beach of sorts – a good place to run the dog and catch a tan – it's both closer and far sunnier than the city's "real" beaches.

You'll see lots of churches around here, but the Moorish-looking structure across the park is the public Mission High School.

2 **Walk down towards the lefthand centre of the park to the statue of Miguel Hidalgo (1753-1811).**

Until the 1840s, California "belonged" first to Spain and then to Mexico. Hidalgo was a hero of the fight for Mexican independence from Spain.

3 **Backtrack towards the southern boundary of the park, emerging at 20th Street and Dolores. Cross Dolores Street and continue along 20th.**

The 1906 fires stopped here at 20th Street. Houses on your left were built (or moved here) after the fire. On your right are examples of houses built in the late 1800s that survived the fire. (You'll see even better examples of pre-fire houses as you continue walking.)

OPPOSITE: DOLORES PARK, WITH SPECTACULAR VIEWS OF DOWNTOWN; ABOVE: STATUE OF MIGUEL HIDALGO

DISTANCE 2 miles (3.2km) – a few hills

ALLOW 3 hours, or 4 if you spend time in the Mission chapel and cemetery

START 20th Street and Church Street

FINISH 16th Street and Church Street

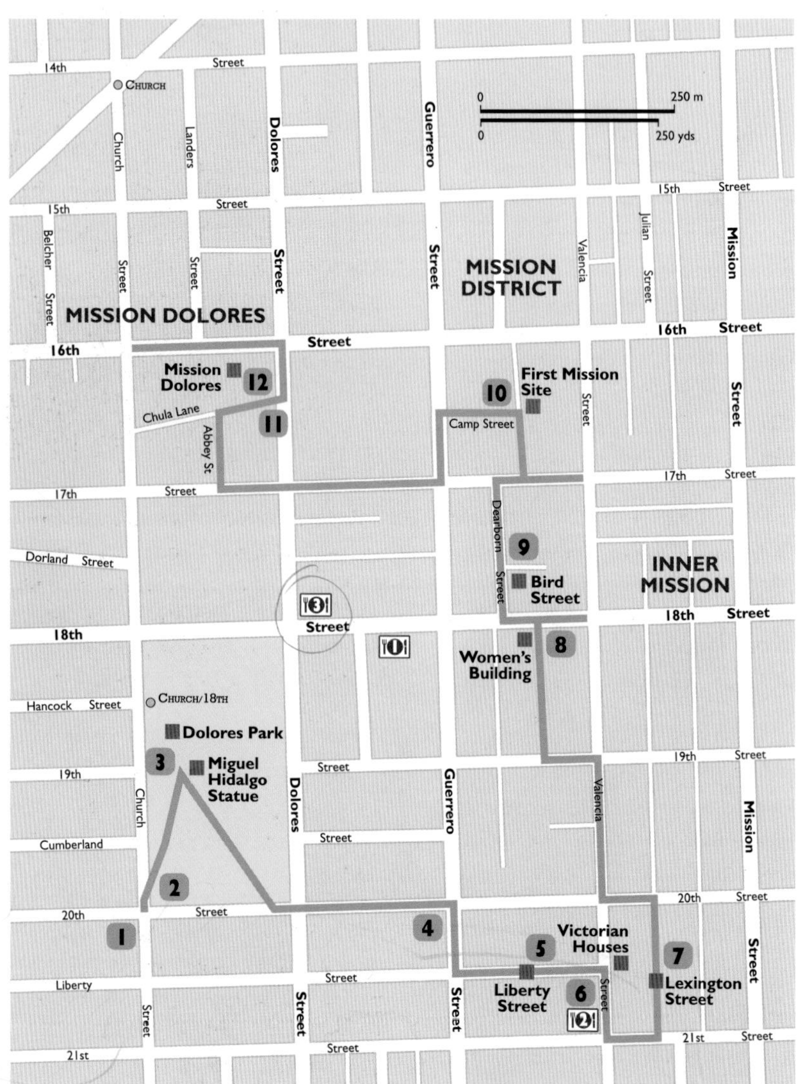

4 At Guerrero, cross and turn right, walking uphill to Liberty Street. Turn left on Liberty.

Enjoy the stroll down this historic district of mostly architect-designed homes from the 1870s and 1880s.

5 Continue on Liberty to Valencia Street. Stop at the corner and look at the cluster of four Victorian houses across the street.

This cluster was the making of The Real Estate Associates (TREA) company, one of the most prolific builders of affordable housing in the 1870s. They bought up several blocks here and built dozens of nearly identical houses, each on a tiny lot. (See more on TREA in Walk 13.)

6 Turn right on Valencia, then left on 21st Street. Turn left on Lexington.

Two blocks behind you, along Bartlett Street near 23rd Street, is the site of the city's most famous dual murder. In early April 1895, the bodies of first one young woman and then another were found raped and stabbed (one in the library, one in the belfry) in what was then the Emmanuel Baptist Church. The murderer (Theo Durrant) and both victims (Blanche Lamont and Minnie Williams) were all active members of the church. Through arrest, trials and appeals, Durrant claimed no recollection of the events, and insisted on his innocence, despite overwhelming evidence against him. He was hanged on 7 January 1898.

WHERE TO EAT

1 DELFINA,
3621 18th Street;
Tel: 1-415-552-4055.
Get a full dinner here, or have lighter fare at Pizzeria Delfina next door. $$

2 MISSION CREEK CAFÉ,
968 Valencia Street;
Tel: 1-415-641-0888.
Relaxed atmosphere, and a good place to sit and people watch. $

3 BI-RITE CREAMERY,
3692 18th Street;
Tel: 1-415-626-5600.
Arguably the best ice cream in San Francisco. $

7 Continue past more TREA homes on Lexington Street, turn left on 20th and right on Valencia. Walk to 19th Street, turn left, then right on Lapidge Street, to 18th Street. Stop at the Women's Building, 3543 18th Street at Lapidge.

Following the feminist movement of the 1970s, local women bought what had been a men's gymnasium and drinking centre and turned it into a safe and supportive place for women to gather. When they had paid off their mortgage, they commissioned the murals celebrating the healing power of women.

WOMEN'S BUILDING;
3543 18TH STREET AT LAPIDGE;
www.womensbuilding.org

8 Turn right on 18th Street to the corner of Valencia Street. Cross the street and backtrack on 18th to Dearborn Street. (Be careful crossing 18th: cars don't stop for pedestrians except at major intersections, where there are stop lights and crossings.) Turn right on Dearborn and continue to Bird.

Along 18th Street, you are walking on water – can you feel it? The creek that comes down from Twin Peaks runs underground now but it used to feed a lagoon here that was a favourite spot for Native Americans to hunt migratory birds. In 1906, a hotel at 18th and Valencia collapsed in the quake – residents should have been able to escape but many were trapped and drowned as broken water mains filled the underground creek. Local businesses report the creek is still here – their basements cannot be pumped dry.

With its great micro-climate, this is a good area for gardens. The one at Bird and Dearborn is a community garden, with individuals or families each caring for a specific section.

9 Continue on Dearborn to 17th Street. Walk to the corner along 17th Street, cross over and backtrack to Albion. (Be careful crossing Valencia.) On the right side of the street, at the corner of Camp Street, stop at the plaque commemorating the first site of the mission.

The Franciscans' first choice for a mission site was here, at the lagoon that provided water, food – and Native Americans who came to hunt and fish. A few wet winters proved their first choice too close to the water, which is why they moved uphill, where their permanent chapel still exists.

10 Turn left on Camp Street, left again on Guerrero, and right on 17th Street. Continue to Abbey Street, turn right, then right again on Chula Lane.

You're walking over an old cemetery that includes the unmarked graves of thousands of Native Americans. Be sure to peek through the fence to the still-maintained cemetery with marked graves of European-descended early settlers.

11 Turn left on Dolores to the old adobe Mission Dolores Chapel.

As you enter, pick up a guide to the 18th-century chapel, the museum in the back, and the cemetery. This is one of two cemeteries still in San Francisco (the other is at the Presidio). The grave that "Carlotta" and Scottie visited in Hitchcock's *Vertigo* isn't here (it never was) but that of gold-rush era madam Belle Cora is. It's faded, but look out for the headstone of Charles and Annabelle Cora: with your back to the gift shop, it's ahead and to the left about two-thirds of the way along to the back fence.

www.missiondolores.org

12 To return to the J-Church street car, as you exit the chapel, turn left on Dolores Street, then left again on 16th Street. Church Street and the J-Church street car are one block up.

OPPOSITE: 18TH-CENTURY MISSION DOLORES CHAPEL AND 20TH-CENTURY BASILICA

MURAL ON THE WOMEN'S BUILDING, CELEBRATING THE HEALING POWER OF WOMEN

ALEJANDRINA
DYLCIA PAGÁN
NOSOTRAS
RODRIGUEZ

WALK 17

Coming out in Castro, the End of Town

In the late 19th century, the area known as The Castro marked the end of town. In the late 20th century, it became a haven for gay culture.

Officially called Eureka Valley, this used to be the end of the world. Market Street stopped here. Dairy cows grazed. In 1887, a cable car line extended along Market, then up and over the Castro Street hill, and Irish immigrants started claiming the area as their own. A trolley tunnel under Twin Peaks opened in 1917, and this was no longer the end of the world. As time went by, long-time residents started retiring to the suburbs. Home ownership dropped, and so did rents. In 1964, *Life* magazine declared San Francisco "the capital of the gay world" but at that time it was referring to North Beach and along Polk Street. By 1977, when Castro Street businessman Harvey Milk was elected city supervisor, the neighbourhood – now called The Castro – had become known as a safe place for gays to be "out". Reaction to Milk's assassination in 1978 and the devastation of the HIV-AIDS epidemic (since 1981), has created a strong sense of community pride and camaraderie. On this walk, you'll see proof of this in flags and homes, but you'll also see evidence of times when this was the beginning of nowhere.

1 Take the underground Muni train K, L, M, S or T to Castro station. Or take the historic F-Castro street car. At the corner of Market Street and Castro Street, visit the Rainbow Flag, and go downstairs in the Muni station to Harvey Milk Plaza.

Rainbow flags fly all over the district, but if someone says, "Meet you at the Rainbow Flag," this is the one they mean. It was installed here to commemorate Harvey Milk's election as the first openly gay city supervisor, on 8 November 1977. The politically conservative and closeted Milk had worked on Wall Street until getting involved with the director of the Hippie musical *Hair*, after which he moved to San Francisco and came "out". He opened a camera shop on Castro Street, made friends with customers and other business owners, and soon became the informal "mayor of Castro Street".

Milk became a hero of the gay movement when he was elected, and became a martyr when disgruntled former city supervisor Dan White shot and killed Milk (and Mayor George Moscone) on 27 November 1978. On the night of the assassination, 20,000 people marched with candles to City Hall. In the trial, White's attorneys launched the now-famous "Twinkie defence", claiming that the junk food he'd consumed made him act irrationally. Much to the outrage of the community, White was not convicted of murder but of the lighter charge of manslaughter.

2 As you exit Harvey Milk Plaza, turn right down Castro Street. This block includes some of the many thriving businesses in The Castro. Look across, for example at:

Twin Peaks Tavern, 401 Castro, at the corner of 17th Street. The first gay bar to have plate glass windows – no need to hide in dark corners any more!

Castro Theatre, 429 Castro: a rare survivor of the old movie palaces. Built in 1922 by architect Timothy Pflueger (1892-1946), it presents mostly foreign and off-beat films, and is home to several film festivals. The mighty Wurlitzer organ still rises in a fantasy interior.

Cliff's Variety Store, 479 Castro: selling everything from plumbing fixtures to feather boas, this store dates from 1936.

3 To see the site of Harvey Milk's home and camera shop (it is no longer either), pass 18th Street and look for 573-575 Castro, on the left. Then backtrack to 18th Street and turn left.

At the corner, Harvey's, 500 Castro, is a popular bar that was used for some on-location filming in the movie *Milk*, starring Sean Penn.

4 Continue up 18th Street. At Diamond, turn left. You're at Most Holy Redeemer Roman Catholic Church, 100 Diamond Street.

When it was founded (1901), this was the anchor of Eureka Valley's Irish Catholic immigrant community.

OPPOSITE: CASTRO THEATRE, BUILT IN 1922, IS ONE OF THE FEW SURVIVING OLD MOVIE PALACES

DISTANCE 1.5 miles (2.5km) – some hills and stairs

ALLOW 1.5 hours

START Castro Muni Station

FINISH Market Street

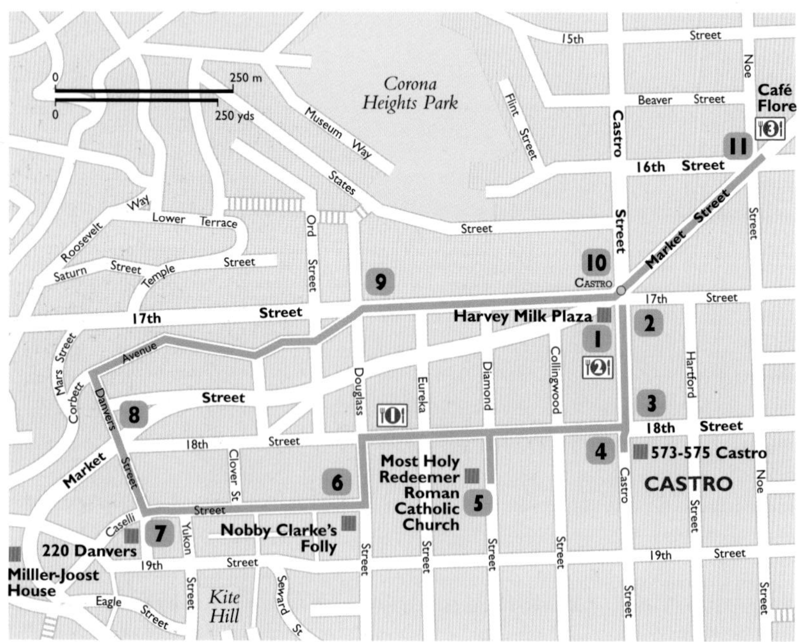

Moving with the times, it now openly embraces the gay community and offers active support in the form of an AIDS-HIV help group and a hospice.

5 Backtrack to 18th and continue to Douglass Street. Turn left. At the next corner, across the street to your right is Nobby Clarke's Folly, 250 Douglass.

In an era when most homes cost $3,000 to $5,000, Alfred "Nobby" Clarke spent $100,000 on 17 acres of land and this four-storey multi-towered home. He was gambling that the area would improve now that the cable car came out to Castro Street. He'd sailed from his native Ireland to California along with so many other teenagers during the gold rush, but returned to the city to work as a stevedore. He soon found he could earn even more at the police department. Indeed, in his position as clerk to the Chief of Police, he managed to save $200,000 (one assumes he had

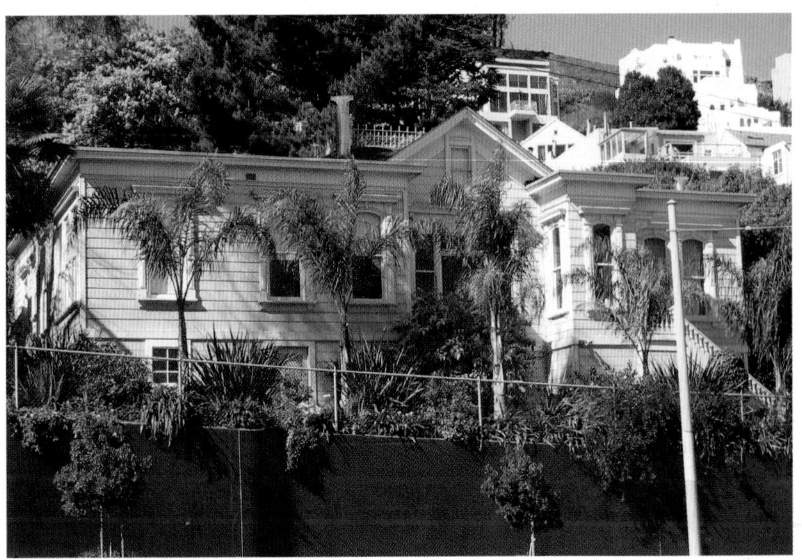

sources other than his salary). But, while he believed in the neighbourhood, his wife and son were not convinced. They wanted to be with the other rich folk, on Nob Hill (thus the origin of his sobriquet), not stuck out here at the end of the world! The family stayed only a few years. The house has since been a hospital, a rooming house for Standard Oil employees, and is now subdivided into apartments and offices.

6 Turn right here on Caselli Street and walk up Caselli to Danvers Street. On your left, across the street is 220 Danvers.

Now a private residence, this was until recently home of progressive Reform Congregation Sha'ar Zahav's synagogue. Started in 1977, the membership outgrew this space and recently moved to a new location at 290 Dolores Street, across from Mission Dolores.

7 Turn right on Danvers. Cross Market Street.

Uphill past the mural on the right, the pink farmhouse that now faces you on Market Street is the Miller-Joost house. Dating from 1867, it is the oldest house in the area. The original owner, dairyman Adam Miller, grazed his cattle on the hill where Corbett Avenue is now. (You'll be there in a moment.) When Miller's daughter Anna married German immigrant Behrend Joost, Miller gave them the house and moved out. Hardworking Joost had started as a store clerk, put his savings into real estate, and owned grocery stores. After he moved here, he purchased the franchise for an electric train line over the hill. He

ABOVE: THE MILLER-JOOST HOUSE, BUILT IN 1867 WHEN ALL AROUND WAS FARMLAND

WHERE TO EAT

1 QUEEN MALIKA,
4416 18th Street;
Tel: 1-415-626-4416.
Great crepes and pastries. Off the beaten track. $

2 MARCELLO'S PIZZA,
420 Castro Street;
Tel: 1-415-863-3900.
Buy a whole pizza or a slice. One of many options along Castro Street. $

3 CAFÉ FLORE,
2298 Market Street;
Tel: 1-415-621-8579.
Come here for coffee – or come just to see and be seen. $$

also tapped a local spring and created Mountain Spring Water Company. Once friends, he and Nobby Clarke became arch enemies – the spring had flowed through Clarke's land but now it didn't. Embittered and apparently estranged from his family, on 24 September 1917 Joost committed suicide, to avoid a slow death by old age and disease (he was 82).

8 Continue up Danvers until it ends at Corbett Avenue. Turn right on Corbett.

When this was the edge of town, streets were unpaved, and houses were scattered up the hillsides. Later, when hills were graded to make streets, some houses were left dangling above- or below-grade. Note the lengthy staircases in front of 242 and 238 Corbett, as Danvers meets Corbett Avenue.

9 When Corbett Avenue merges with 17th Street, continue along 17th Street until just before you get back to the Market and Castro intersection.

On the left is the McCormick House (built 1902) with the onion dome, at 4040-4042 17th Street. On the right is the Pink Triangle Park and Memorial at 17th and Castro. A lovely triangular mini-park with pink quartz gravel and triangular granite columns commemorating both gay pride and victims of AIDS. (In Nazi concentration camps, homosexual prisoners were made to wear an inverted pink triangle badge as identification – now a pink triangle is a badge of righteous pride.)

10 With the Rainbow Flag across Market Street on your right, cross Castro Street and veer left on to Market Street.

2348 Market Street is the site (no longer there) of the first openly gay bar in this area: the Missouri Mule, opened in 1963. At the next corner is Café Flore, 2298 Market Street, a place to sit back and enjoy life.

11 When you're ready to finish the walk, take the F-Market street car across the street, or walk back to Castro and Market to catch the underground Muni train.

OPPOSITE: PINK TRIANGLE PARK AND MEMORIAL, COMMEMORATING GAY PRIDE AND AIDS VICTIMS

WALK 18

Love and Headstones in Haight-Ashbury

Haight-Ashbury, at the edge of Golden Gate Park – this is where the dead are not remembered, but the hippies and psychedelia are!

What had been a turn-of-the-century upscale neighbourhood became run-down by the 1930s Depression years, then crowded in the 1940s war years, with many single-family houses subdivided into flats. By the 1950s and 1960s, it was decidedly dilapidated. So, when young folk flocked to the city to join the Beat culture (see Walk 7) and found North Beach too crowded, many landed here. And then, counter-culture happened. Crash pads were common, as was "free love". Many well-known bands played free concerts in the park. Bill Graham started producing concerts with pulsing rock rhythms, psychedelic posters, light shows, LSD and marijuana – and free apples. A fascinating district in its own right, Haight-Ashbury is steeped in nostalgia for the 1967 Summer of Love, when as many as 100,000 converged here, at the heart of the hippie revolution. On this walk, encounter headstones in the park, the houses where the Hells Angels lived and those of mass murderer Charles Manson and rocker Janis Joplin, and the house where ballet phenomenon Rudolph Nureyev (1938-93) was busted for pot.

1 Get off the No. 6 Muni bus at Haight Street and Central Avenue. Turn right down Central Avenue past 142 Central, where there used to be a recording studio in the basement. Then continue to the park.

The Panhandle is the one-block wide strip of park that extends eastward for eight additional blocks after the main section of Golden Gate Park ends at Stanyan Street. In the 1960s, it was a place for "be-ins" and impromptu concerts.

2 At Oak Street, facing the park, turn right, then right again on Lyon Street.

Janis Joplin lived for a while in the house at 122 Lyon. Only 27 when she died in 1970, Janis's heartfelt, gravel-voiced blues-rock vocals (*Piece of My Heart, Ball and Chain, Get It While You Can*) made her a superstar, singing with Big Brother and the Holding Company.

3 Continue up Lyon Street and climb the wide cement stairs to enter Buena Vista Park. There are many pathways through Buena Vista, but to see gravestones (without attached bodies) proceed this way. At the top of the stairs, bear left. At the first crossing (5 points), take the top left path. At the next crossing, you'll see a storage building in front of you. Take the uppermost path on the right.

As you walk, look at the dressed stone in the retaining walls and the storm gutters. When the city forced the removal of cemeteries from within city limits, *most* graves and gravestones were moved to nearby Colma – but if the dead hadn't left a hefty bequest, or if family members couldn't be found, bones, caskets and headstones were left behind. When, in the 1930s, the anti-Depression Works Progress Administration paved the paths in the park, they lined the gutters and

OPPOSITE: HIPPIE SHOPPING; ABOVE: PATH MADE FROM BROKEN GRAVESTONES AT BUENA VISTA PARK

DISTANCE **2.6 miles (4.2km) – some hills and stairs**

ALLOW **2 hours**

START **Haight Street and Central Avenue**

FINISH **Haight Street**

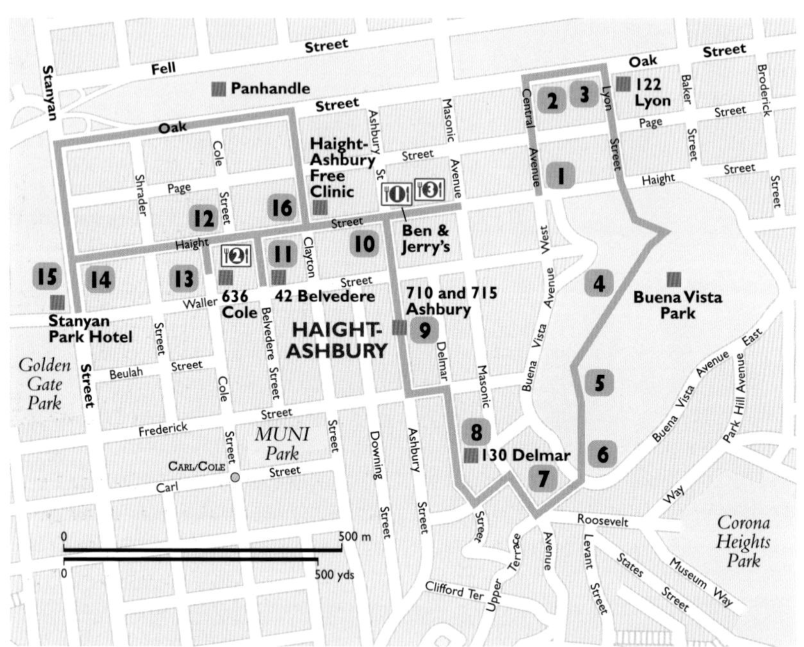

walls with dressed granite and headstones (nearly all face down) from left-over graves from Lone Mountain Cemetery.

4 At the next crossing (4 points), again take the uppermost path on the right. Continue on this path as it curves and heads generally uphill.

When the path opens through a clearing, just past clumps of redwood trees, you'll spy the most recognizable piece of headstone in the park, at the base of the retaining wall. Was Mary Anne's last name Conroy or Conway? If you don't find her grave, don't fret. Sometimes Mary Anne seems to go into hiding, and even those who know the park well cannot find her.

5 At the next crossing, a T junction, stay to the left.

When the view opens up on your right, pause to catch your breath. The red-roofed tower and buildings in front of the bridge are at the location of the original

Lone Mountain Cemetery; Masonic Cemetery (Emperor Norton's burial site) was between Lone Mountain and the two-spired church (St Ignatius), to the west.

6 Continuing on the path, bear right at the fork then stay on this path until it takes you out of the park at Buena Vista Avenue and Upper Terrace Street. Cross Buena Vista Avenue and walk one block downhill on Upper Terrace.

Rock star Graham Nash, of Crosby, Stills, Nash and Young, has lived in this neighbourhood (and helped produce recordings of the Quick Silver Messenger Service and the Steve Miller Band in his basement recording studio). Also in the area is Lemony Snicket, author of *A Series of Unfortunate Events*. The red clinker brick house at 45 Upper Terrace is said to have been a Japanese consulate and also to be haunted, but apparently neither tale is true.

7 Turn right for one block on Masonic Avenue. Turn left on Piedmont. Turn right on Delmar Street to 130 Delmar.

The rock band Jefferson Airplane – with hits like *White Rabbit* and *Plastic Fantastic Lover* – lived in this house during the Summer of Love. (After the success of *Surrealistic Pillow*, they purchased the former lumber baron's mansion at 2400 Fulton Street to serve as home, office and recording studio.)

WHERE TO EAT

1 BEN & JERRY'S,
Corner of Haight and Ashbury;
Tel: 1-415-626-4143.
A branch of the ice cream company started by two friends in Vermont. $

2 RED VIC PEACE CAFÉ
1665 Haight Street;
Tel: 1-415-864-1978.
A fun meander into history. $

3 BLUE FRONT DELI & CAFÉ,
1430 Haight Street;
Tel: 1-415-252-5917.
A local favourite, serving light snacks and hearty meals. $

8 Continue downhill on Delmar. Turn left on Frederick Street. Turn right on Ashbury Street. Mid-block, you'll see these two houses across the street from each other:

710 Ashbury was the 1966-68 home of the band Grateful Dead, who mixed rock with reggae, blues, folk and country and became the quintessential San Francisco Sound. Their fans are "Deadheads".

715 Ashbury was former headquarters of the San Francisco Hells Angels, sometime-outlaw motorcyclists who gained fame in the rock world when their "security" activities at the December 1969 Altamont Speedway Free Festival – featuring the Rolling Stones, Santana, Jefferson Airplane and others – turned deadly.

9 Continue on Ashbury to the corner of Haight Street.

This is the intersection that gave the culture a name. Ben & Jerry's, now part of a larger corporation, started when two old hippie friends in Vermont began making ice cream, then blended ice cream with social activism.

10 Turn left on Haight Street and walk through memory lane. At Belvedere Street, turn left.

42 Belvedere is the address where Russian ballet dancer Rudolph Nureyev (1938-93) was arrested for smoking marijuana in July 1967 after neighbours had called the police complaining of a noisy party. The charges against Nureyev were later dropped.

11 Backtrack to Haight Street and turn left.

Stop at the RedVic Bed, Breakfast and Art at 1655 Haight. Built in 1904 as the Jefferson Hotel, artist and peace pilgrim Sami Sunchild bought the building in 1977 and turned it into a nostalgic B & B reflecting the 1960s.

12 At Cole Street turn left.

636 Cole Street was home to infamous cult leader and murderer Charles Manson and his coterie of women followers. Manson already had a long history of violent crime (burglaries, car theft, pimping) and had spent time in prison when he came here in 1967 because he'd heard there was "free love".

13 Backtrack to Haight Street, and turn left again.

You'll walk by the amazing music store Amoeba Music, at 1855 Haight, housed in a building that was once a bowling alley. If the weather is good, detour into Golden Gate Park at this point. Duck through the tunnel to Hippie Hill, site of many a 1960s "be-in" or "happening". Then backtrack.

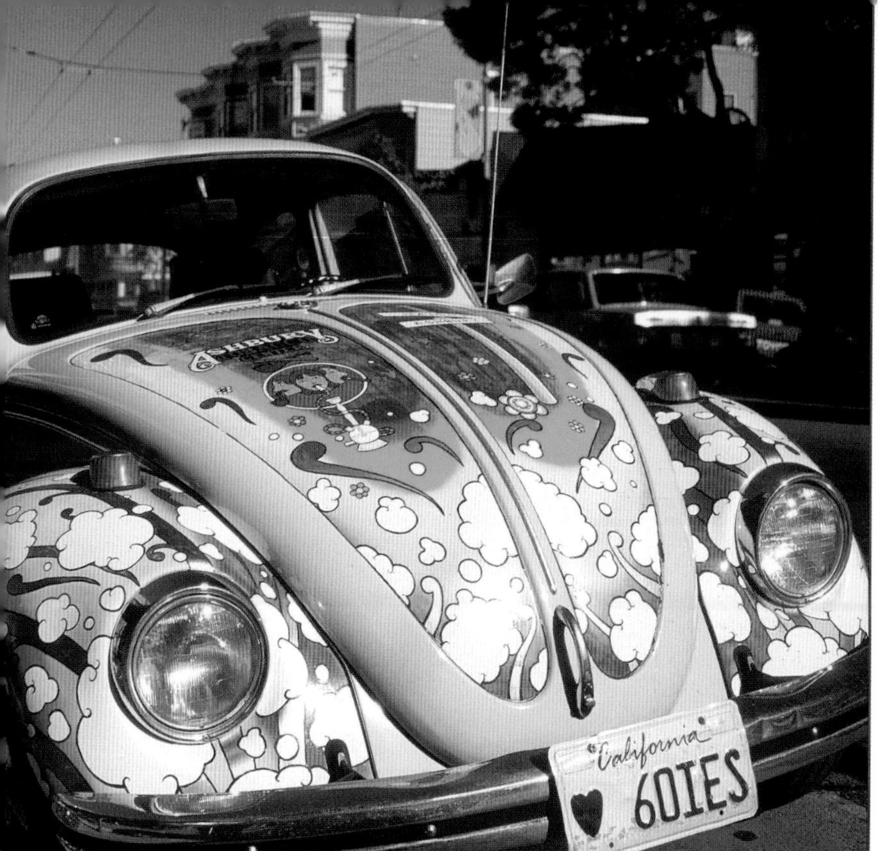

14 At the end of Haight Street, turn left on Stanyan Street.

The historic Stanyan Park Hotel, at 750 Stanyan, was built in 1904.

15 Backtrack on Stanyan along Golden Gate Park and continue to Oak Street. Turn right, and either walk along Oak, or walk back through the Panhandle. At Clayton Street, turn right.

558 Clayton is the historic site of the Haight-Ashbury Free Clinic, founded in June 1967 to provide a safe place for patients needing help with drug, alcohol or other medical problems. The clinic is also famous for its mobile RockMed program, created in 1973 when rock promoter Bill Graham asked it to staff emergency services at Grateful Dead and Led Zeppelin outdoor concerts, and is now active at concerts, marches, celebrations and fairs.

16 Turn left on Haight Street and continue to enjoy the sights and sounds, at least as far as Masonic Avenue. Catch the No. 6 Muni bus at any bus stop along the way.

ABOVE: A CUSTOMIZED BEETLE CONTINUES HAIGHT-ASHBURY'S LOVE AFFAIR WITH THE SIXTIES

NICE PAIR OF LEGS: FANCIFUL SCULPTURE ON HAIGHT STREET

ASHBURY
1600 →
HAIGHT

WALK 19

Golden Gate Park – the Park that Pride Built

Walk through the manicured eastern end of Golden Gate Park, the city's heart and lungs. See fine art, exotic plants, an asteroid and maybe a ghost.

When New York got its Central Park, San Francisco wanted one too. Central Park's landscape architect Frederick Law Olmsted refused an offer to create a design, saying it couldn't be done! No land had been set aside for a park. The city convinced squatters to part with a portion of their holdings, thus a space half a mile wide and three miles long was secured – but what would secure the shifting shoreline and sand dunes? Ingenuity, tenacity and an accident with a horse's feedbag (spilled barley grew sufficient roots to allow lupins and other plants to grow) made it happen. It was turned into an accessible people's park, with curving paths, a ban on cars (so as not to scare the horses and cyclists), natural areas and no "Keep off the grass" signs. Then, two decades after the transformation began, rivalry and civic pride helped boost the park again, when San Francisco businessman Michael de Young created a world's fair to compete with Chicago's 1893 Columbian Exposition. Visit any day except Mondays, when the de Young Museum and Conservatory of Flowers are closed.

1 **Get off the N-Judah street car at 9th Avenue. Turn downhill on 9th Avenue towards the park and continue into the park. After the first building on your left, follow the signs to the Strybing Arboretum.**

A stroll through this living museum of plants is like a mini world tour, with plantlife from all parts of the globe.

Megalomaniac newspaper tycoon William Randolph Hearst (1863-1951), model for *Citizen Kane* by Orson Welles, was at least partially responsible for the beautiful stonework next to the horticultural library. In 1931, Hearst fell in love with the Cistercian abbey of Santa Maria de Ovila (built from the 12th to the 17th century), and declared that it should be disassembled from its perch above the Tagus River in Spain, brought to California, and reassembled on one of Hearst's estates. Some 10,000 stones – which had made up the chapel, refectory, chapter house, arcaded cloister and church door portal – were coded, dismantled, crated and shipped to San Francisco. Once here, the crates were warehoused while architects worked on designs for the estate. By this time, Hearst had run out of money and offered the crates to the city (in return for generous financial compensation). But the story isn't over yet. At some point, fires burned through the warehouses, destroying the crates and the codes for reassembling the pieces, along with many of the stones. After more years of abuse, neglect and dispersion, the stones that remained were crafted into this lovely terrace.

STRYBING ARBORETUM;
www.sfbotanicalgarden.org

2 **Cross the road you came in on and turn onto Concourse Drive. (How you get to Concourse Drive depends on where you leave the arboretum. If you leave the arboretum where you entered, you should turn left on the main road – Martin Luther King Junior Drive – then**

OPPOSITE: CONSERVATORY OF FLOWERS; ABOVE: STRYBING ARBORETUM

DISTANCE **4 miles (6.5km)**

ALLOW **2-3 hours, or all day if you spend time in any of the museums**

START **9th Avenue at Irving or Judah**

FINISH **9th Avenue at Irving or Judah**

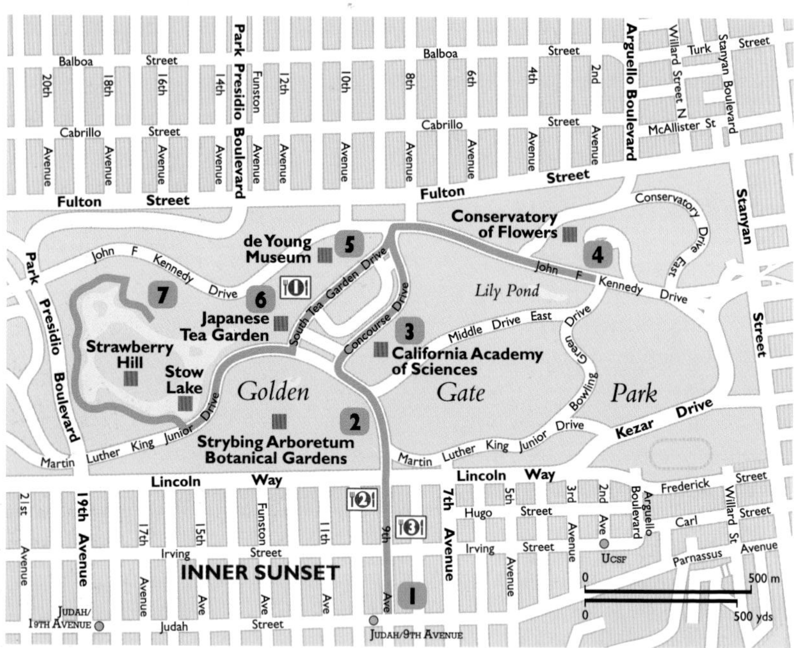

turn right into Concourse Drive. If you leave the arboretum further along, turn right on the main road, then left into Concourse Drive.) On your left is the tree-lined open space of the Music Concourse, and on your right is the California Academy of Sciences.

This brand new environmentally "green" building, with a living roof and many other sustainable features, is home to the oldest scientific institution in the western US (founded in 1853). In its early days, Charles Darwin (1809-82) was a corresponding fellow. The academy moved to this location after its downtown headquarters were destroyed in the 1906 earthquake and fire. Over the next hundred years, new elements were added until eventually the building no longer fit its purpose. So, all the animals were transported across town to a temporary facility, and then back again to the new one – imagine moving penguins, snakes, alligators, coral and sea bass. How did they do it? Canvas bags for the snakes, stretchers for the sea bass, dog carriers for the penguins – and the trucks were driven very slowly so the water wouldn't slosh out! Read their stories at the academy, or just check out the Amazon flooded forest, multi-storied coral reef, the swamp, the planetarium and the natural history museum.

CALIFORNIA ACADEMY OF SCIENCES;
www.calacademy.org.

3 As you exit the academy, turn right along the road, then right again at John F Kennedy Drive. Cross to your left, and when you see the Conservatory of Flowers, walk up the entry path to it.

Eccentric millionaire James Lick (see Walk 1) had commissioned greenhouses for his private estate but died before they

WHERE TO EAT

1 JAPANESE TEA GARDEN,
Golden Gate Park;
Tel: 1-415-752-4227.
Tea and fortune cookies in a peaceful setting. $$

2 LITTLE SHAMROCK PUB,
807 Lincoln Way at 9th Avenue;
Tel: 1-415-661-0060.
Opened to satisfy the thirsts of Irish labourers who came to build the 1894 Fair. $$

3 PARK CHOW,
1240 9th Avenue;
Tel: 1-415-665-9912.
Serves light and full meals. $$

ABOVE: THE CALIFORNIA ACADEMY OF SCIENCES WITH ITS LIVING ROOF OF NATIVE PLANTS

could be assembled. As with Hearst's Cistercian abbey, Lick's greenhouses were given to San Francisco in pieces, then transformed into what became the Conservatory of Flowers. The designers took inspiration from the Palm House in London's Kew Gardens when making this structure.

As you walk through the park, notice the absence of "Keep off the grass" signs. Early park superintendent Scotsman John McLaren insisted that visitors walk on the grass. In fact, had you been here in the 1890s, you might have seen otherwise prim Victorians walking barefoot on the grass, shoes and stockings in hand, when every morning at 6.30, hydropathist August Willman's "water therapy" treatments brought his followers from the dirty inner city to be cleansed by the morning dew.

CONSERVATORY OF FLOWERS;
www.conservatoryofflowers.org

4 Leaving the conservatory, backtrack on John F Kennedy Drive, and into the concourse area again, on Tea Garden Drive. On your right is the de Young Museum.

The de Young Museum was an exotic Egyptian-style building recycled from the 1894 Midwinter Fair, held to compete with Chicago, following that city's successful 1893 Columbian Exposition. To promote San Francisco's salubrious winter climate, its fair started on 1 January. Was it mere coincidence that the fair's main backer – newspaper editor Michael de Young – owned undeveloped real estate nearby, real estate whose value would rise with increased local traffic?

The century-old museum was already straining at its limits when a major earthquake in 1989 caused sufficient structural damage that complete reconstruction was in order. Critics argued that the museum didn't belong in the park and should have been removed altogether. Views differ on whether the new design, with its undulating exhibition spaces and dark view tower, enhances or ruins the park.

DE YOUNG MUSEUM;
www.famsf.org/deyoung

5 As you exit the museum, turn right. On your right is the Japanese Tea Garden.

Originally created as the Japanese Village for the 1894 Midwinter Fair, the tea garden was inspired by a similar exhibit in the Chicago Exposition. After the fair, Osaka-born landscape gardener Makoto Hagiwara lived here with his family until his death in 1925, and expanded and moulded it into its current state. Daughter Tanako Hagiwara took over from her father until she and her family were forced to leave for a wartime internment camp in Utah in 1941 (see Walk 14). By the way, along with the tea that the Hagiwaras always served to visitors here were sweet folded cookies with a fortune inside. These somehow made their way to Chinatown and became "Chinese" fortune cookies!

JAPANESE TEA GARDEN;
www.sfpt.org/japanese_tea_garden.html

6 As you exit the Tea Garden, turn right, then, at the main road, turn right again. Walk around the bend and follow signs to Stow Lake on the road uphill on your right.

Strawberry Hill, the island in the middle of the lake, is a natural stone outcropping originally covered by sand – this wouldn't be remarkable except that it is one of the few natural features in the park. Stow Lake itself is a man-made reservoir. As you walk around, you'll pass pump-fed Huntington Falls. The Roman Bridge connecting the outer path to the island isn't Roman at all, of course. The Chinese Pavilion was imported in pieces from Taipei. Even with its elements of a stage set, this is a relaxing place that you'll share with walkers, joggers, cyclists, kids watching the turtles sunning themselves, and those who've rented paddle boats at the boathouse.

You'll also share the island with the ghost of a woman who is said to have drowned her unwanted infant here – the ghost is sad but friendly. She comes here regretting the tragedy that shaped her life.

7 When you've finished enjoying the park for the day, backtrack downhill and around to the left on Martin Luther King Junior Drive, back to 9th Avenue and Irving for the N-Judah street car.

ABOVE: THE JAPANESE TEA GARDEN IN GOLDEN GATE PARK

WALK 20

Ships and Shellfish on Fisherman's Wharf

A walk through Fisherman's Wharf, where tourists and fishermen have rubbed shoulders on the piers and in the bars for well over a century.

Fisherman's Wharf is traditionally a centre for fishermen and their boats. The 19th century's fishing fleet – Chinese junks, Italian *feluccas* and other sailboats – gave way in the 20th century to motorized vessels. Recently, overfishing and other challenges helped shift the balance from fishing to tourism. But tourism began as far back as 1856, when Abe Warner built his "Cobweb Palace" on the old wharf. Sailors, sea captains and locals came to Abe's to see the scrimshaw of sperm whale teeth and walrus tusks, taxidermists' gems, a menagerie of live parrots and monkeys (plus an occasional bear or kangaroo), all adorned by cobwebs spun by Abe's beloved spiders – and, of course, they came to drink. In 1915, a new kind of cocktail was invented here: the crab cocktail – not a beverage, but a take-away snack. Today, Fisherman's Wharf is still the place to enjoy a crab cocktail, eat clam chowder from a sourdough bread bowl and experience San Francisco chocolate. You can also visit a haunted ship, have your fortune told, and walk through a park made of leftovers from the old city.

1 **Take the Hyde Street cable car to the terminus at Hyde Street at Beach. As you face the bay, turn left on Beach Street, and walk to Ghirardelli Square, with the massive red brick buildings on your left.**

If you're chilly and it's not too early, stop in at the Buena Vista Café for a warming Irish coffee – they've been making them here since 1952.

Italian chocolate-maker Domenico Ghirardelli arrived in California for the gold rush. By the 1890s, his business outgrew the downtown location so he moved here, taking over the factory buildings of an old woollen mill. The factory moved out in the 1960s, but you can still find chocolate and other delicacies here. Read the historic signs on your way to the ice cream parlour.

2 **Exit Ghirardelli Square at the lower level, cross Beach Street and go into Victoria Park. Turn left by the Maritime Museum, and continue on out to the end of the Municipal Pier.**

If the Maritime Museum is open, be sure to go in. It was built in the 1930s to feel like a luxury cruise ship, and the collection is excellent.

As you walk out to the pier, you are walking over a graveyard of old San Francisco, but no human bodies are buried here – just city rubble. The sand at the beach came from downtown, excavated in the 1930s from under Union Square (while they were building the parking area there). And the park itself sits atop landfill from 1906. The quakes and fires created more than 10 million cubic yards of bricks, boards, pipes, old kitchen debris and the ruins of people's lives. Most should have been dumped at sea but some was left in more accessible places, like right here!

WHERE TO EAT

1 BOUDIN BAKERY,
160 Jefferson Street;
Tel: 1-415-928-1849.
For sandwiches or a baguette to go. $

2 GHIRARDELLI ICE CREAM AND CHOCOLATE SHOP,
Clock Tower Building, Ghirardelli Square;
Tel: 1-415-474-1414.
For all the sweets you can eat. $$

3 BUENA VISTA CAFÉ,
2765 Hyde Street at Beach;
Tel: 1-415-474-5044.
Famous for their Irish coffee. $$

3 **Backtrack along the water's edge past the park all the way to the beach-side buildings that are home to the Dolphin Swimming and Boating Club (502 Jefferson) and the South End Rowing Club (500 Jefferson).**

Anxious for a swim? Not so fast… Members of the Dolphin and South End Clubs swim these waters daily. But, with water temperatures hovering around 50°F (10°C) and tides and currents that

OPPOSITE: CRABS ARE STILL ON THE MENU AT FISHERMAN'S WHARF

DISTANCE 2.3 miles (3.7km)

ALLOW 2 hours – longer if you visit the Maritime Museum or any ships

START Hyde Street cable car terminus at Hyde Street at Beach

FINISH Hyde Street cable car terminus or Jefferson at Jones Street for the F-line street car

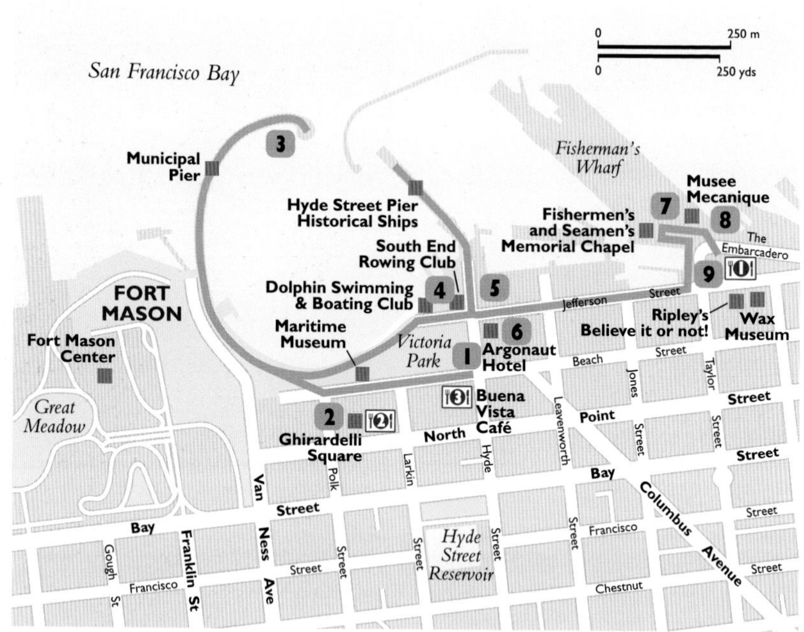

can sweep away the strongest swimmer, you might think twice. The former prison island of Alcatraz ("The Rock") is only 1.5 miles (2.5km) away. In the years it was a federal prison (1934-64), only one inmate was known to swim successfully to the mainland (he was then summarily returned).

Speaking of swimmers, on 27 August 1875, bank president and Palace Hotel backer William C Ralston swam out into the bay, as was his daily custom – but this time he never swam back in. It had been a bad week. Investments had turned sour, and borrowing from one was no longer sufficient to pay off the others. His Bank of California closed its doors after depositors withdrew $1.4 million in a single day. Ralston resigned as bank president. Perhaps he swam out too far, perhaps he suffered a heart attack, perhaps his death was self-induced – we will never know. Thirty-two years later, Harry Houdini (1874-1926) had himself

wrapped in chains and thrown into the water to commemorate Ralston. Unlike Ralston (whose chains were more psychological than physical), Houdini emerged very much alive, after 57 seconds under water.

4 A short way ahead, turn left on the Hyde Street Pier. Among the historic vessels along the pier are a paddlewheel tug, a steam tug, two schooners, a ferryboat and, the prize, an 1886 square-rigger called the *Balclutha*.

Originally launched near Glasgow, Scotland, this three-masted ship carried cargo around the world – 17 trips were around Cape Horn. After retirement, it appeared in the 1935 film *Mutiny on the Bounty*. They say the *Balclutha* is haunted – sailors lost at sea, do you think? Or one of the mutineers? Or perhaps that's just the creaking of wood and ropes.

BALCLUTHA;
www.nps.gov/safr/historyculture/historic-vessels.htm

5 As you exit the pier, cross the street to the Visitor Center of the San Francisco Maritime National Historical Park, at the Argonaut Hotel, 495 Jefferson Street.

The hotel is located in the Cannery building, home from 1907 to fruit packers

ABOVE: THE SQUARE-RIGGER *BALCLUTHA*, SAID TO BE HAUNTED

and, eventually to the Del Monte peach cannery (once the largest in the world). As a state, California produces a cornucopia of farm products, but as a city, San Francisco produces almost none. The city's importance has been as a port, a financial centre and, until recently, a processing centre. Read about the history of the Cannery in the posted signs and displays.

SAN FRANCISCO MARITIME NATIONAL HISTORICAL PARK;

www.argonauthotel.com/argmari

6 When you exit the museum and hotel, backtrack across Jefferson Street and turn right. After walking by restaurants and warehouses on your left (including Alioto-Lazio, a women-owned business where you can get up close and personal with live crabs – www.crabonline.com), the street continues past a small marina of working boats. Just before you get to Tarantino's restaurant, turn left on a brick path that takes you out towards the marina. Turn left again on the wooden pier that heads towards the Fishermen's and Seamen's Memorial Chapel.

A memorial to the fishermen who have lost their lives at sea. On Sunday mornings, you might hear the Gregorian chant of the Divine Office or the traditional Roman Catholic Mass in Latin. If you visit on the first Saturday in October, you will witness the annual blessing of the fleet

FISHERMEN'S AND SEAMEN'S MEMORIAL CHAPEL;

www.traditio.com/stjohn/memorial.htm

7 When you exit, continue along the small bridge in front of the chapel, and turn right on the wide roadway in front of the building marked Pier 45, Shed B. At the next building on your left, Pier 45 Shed A, go in for a visit to the Musee Mecanique.

An amazing collection of antique music boxes, arcade games and modern video games – with an emphasis on the antique. "Laffing Sal", with her raucous laugh, greets you at the door but don't overlook the wizard, the gypsy fortune teller and other haunting figures.

MUSEE MECANIQUE;

www.museemechanique.org

8 Leave the Musee Mecanique from the exit opposite where you entered. If you want to visit more sea-going vessels, turn left and head down to the

ABOVE: JOLLY JACK AT THE MUSEE MECANIQUE; OPPOSITE: PIER 39, FAVOURED BY BASKING SEA LIONS

submarine *USS Pampanito* (built 1943), and the "liberty ship" *Jeremiah O'Brien* (a World War II supply ship working the North Atlantic). Then, head back down the pier and cross the street to the Boudin Bakery and Museum.

Learn the secrets of San Francisco sourdough bread by watching the bakers or visiting the museum, or just buy a loaf downstairs and learn by eating.

BOUDIN BAKERY AND MUSEUM;

www.boudinbakery.com

To check out even more of the weird and mysterious, walk over to the Wax Museum or to Ripley's Believe it or Not!

WAX MUSEUM;

145 JEFFERSON STREET; www.waxmuseum.com

RIPLEY'S BELIEVE IT OR NOT!;

115 JEFFERSON STREET; www.ripleysf.com

Or continue along the waterfront to visit the sea lions, the aquarium and other attractions along Pier 39.

PIER 39;

www.pier39.com

9 When you've had your fill, either backtrack along Jefferson Street to the cable car terminus on Hyde Street, or turn left off Jefferson at Jones Street and catch the historic F-line street car.

THE FORMER PRISON ISLAND OF ALCATRAZ

WALK 21

Ghosts and Beautiful People at the Marina

The Marina buzzes with life. On this walk you can watch the beautiful people, see where Ronald Reagan worked, and hear the music of the sea.

The Marina is sandwiched between two former military bases. Fort Mason, where this walk begins, is home to one of the world's best vegetarian restaurants as well as theatres, art and music studios, and museums. It is also haunted by the ghosts of former slaves and of a white man who lost his life in a duel over slavery. At the edge of the other military base, the Presidio, is a seemingly ancient ruin that needs nearly constant maintenance so that it doesn't collapse, an amazing hands-on science museum, and a jetty built on cemetery rubble where you can hear the crash of water through periscopes. In between the two bases, a lagoon hugged the bay, and a refugee camp hugged the lagoon in 1906. In 1915, both the tidal marsh and lagoon were filled in and this became home to the Panama-Pacific International Exposition, celebrating both the opening of the Panama Canal, and San Francisco's phoenix-like recovery from the destruction of 1906. Now, the "beautiful people" use the area for jogging, sailing, playing soccer, and flirting while shopping for groceries.

1 Take the No. 30 Muni bus and get off at Van Ness Avenue and Bay Street. From Bay Street, turn right on Franklin Street to enter the Upper Fort Mason area. After crossing MacArthur Avenue, the old chapel is just to the left. Continue along Franklin Street. At the circular road on the right, Quarters No. 3 is the haunted Haskell House.

This is now a private home, please do not disturb the residents! Over the years, people have reported ghosts and ghostly activities here (pictures knocked off the wall, lights turned on in empty rooms, cold spots). An investigating ghost hunter saw both a tall gentleman dressed in top hat and frock coat, and frightened disorientated black people. Historians say the tall man is likely to be abolitionist Senator David Broderick, who lost his life in a duel in September 1857 with pro-slavery state supreme court justice David Terry. Before the duel and for three days on his death bed, Broderick was staying here with his friend, homeowner Leonides Haskell. Haskell and Broderick had probably worked together to help southern slaves escape to freedom by hiding them in the basement, along the "underground railway" – probably the source of the frightened, disorientated ghosts.

2 Backtrack on Franklin Street. Just beyond the chapel, turn right on MacArthur, in front of the National Park Service Headquarters, and on to the end of the car park, where you'll be looking out over the Great Meadow and (unless there's fog) to fabulous views of the Golden Gate Bridge.

Four decades before Ronald Reagan would be president of the United States, the dashing young second lieutenant is said to have worked in building 201 here – the one that now houses the park headquarters.

In the distance, you can see the orange dome of the Palace of Fine Arts. Had you looked out at any time between late April 1906 and January 1907, you would have seen a bay-side lagoon, and row upon row of army-issue tents pitched in military precision over sandy paths, with a few horses and thousands of residents. This was the Harbor View refugee camp, one of the biggest and toughest in town. Had you looked out at the same view in 1915, you would have seen the Tower of Jewels, the Column of Progress, the Palace of Manufactures, the Palace of Horticulture, the Fountain of Energy. The lagoon was now filled in, and crowded avenues wove through the Panama Pacific International Exposition.

OPPOSITE: VIEW OF THE GOLDEN GATE BRIDGE FROM MARINA GREEN; ABOVE: SIGN TO HASKELL HOUSE

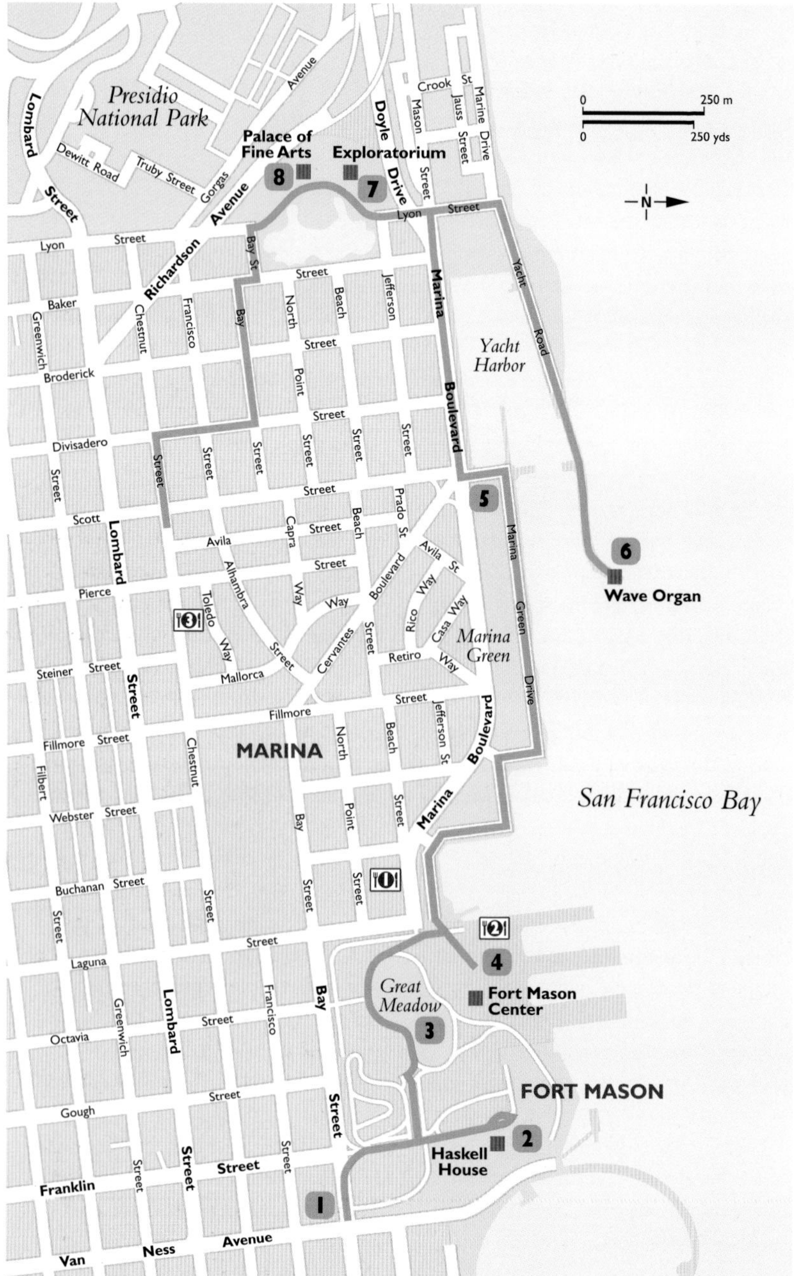
Presidio National Park
Palace of Fine Arts
Exploratorium
Wave Organ
Yacht Harbor
Marina Green
MARINA
San Francisco Bay
Great Meadow
Fort Mason Center
FORT MASON
Haskell House
0
250 m
0
250 yds
N
1
2
3
4
5
6
7
8

DISTANCE 3.5 miles (5.6km)

ALLOW 2.5 hours

START Van Ness Avenue and Bay Street

FINISH Chestnut Street

On 17 October 1989, you would have seen residential houses, much like today, except that flames were shooting skyward from a block built over what had once been the lagoon. The Loma Prieta earthquake caused fires, building collapses and ruptured gas lines. Afterwards, the houses were upgraded and reinforced, the fire department put new fireboats in service, and citizens were taught the skills needed to provide support for firefighters and other disaster relief professionals.

3 Walk down any of the paths through the Great Meadow, heading generally ahead and to the right until you get to the lower section of the park, called Fort Mason Center.

This was the main point of embarkation for the US Army during World War II. Now it is an arts centre, where you can study Italian, learn to sculpt in clay, brush up on your improvisational acting, or attend a new play at the Magic Theatre.

4 As you exit Fort Mason Center, walk along the water's edge, keeping the bay on your right. Turn left and walk through the Marina Green.

The Safeway supermarket across the street is a notorious "pick-up" spot, where he can break the ice by asking her how to tell if a mango is ripe, or they can share recipes for pasta sauce and then decide to cook together.

Historically speaking, you are now walking into the fun, frivolous part of the 1915 Panama-Pacific International Exposition. Amusements and concessions of the "Zone" were grouped together at this end of the fair.

5 At the end of the Marina Green, turn left. At Marina Boulevard turn right. At Lyon Street, turn right, following the signs to the yacht harbour. Continue as the road turns back towards Fort Mason. Through the car park, you pass both the St Francis Yacht Club (1927) and the Golden Gate Yacht Club (1939) to get to the end of the jetty, where you'll find the Wave Organ.

The earphones that pick up the motion of the water are made of periscope-shaped pipes designed to resonate with movement. The steps and platforms and walls are of dressed stone that came from the disassembled Laurel Heights Cemetery. While the Wave Organ is supposed to be a feast for the ears, at low tide the sound can seem muffled – but do not despair. The feast for the eyes more than compensates, with spectacular views to the city, the yacht harbour, Alcatraz and the Golden Gate Bridge.

WHERE TO EAT

1 SAFEWAY,
15 Marina Boulevard;
Tel: 1-415-563-4946.
Where 20-somethings flirt and shop. $

2 GREENS,
Building A, Fort Mason Center;
Tel: 1-415-771-6222.
Even if you're not a vegetarian, the food will delight you (and if you don't want a full meal, they have a take-away counter as well). $$

3 ANDALE MEXICAN RESTAURANT,
2150 Chestnut Street;
Tel: 1-415-749-0506.
A popular option among the many on Chestnut Street. $

In 1900, the City of San Francisco banned further burials in San Francisco (except at Mission Dolores and the Presidio). In 1914, the Board of Health notified known cemetery plot owners of all cemeteries that were to be removed (to the city of Colma, just to the south). Those who chose to exhume and rebury their loved ones could pay to do so, and many – but not all – bodies were indeed moved to Colma. During the Great Depression of the 1930s, the government-funded Works Progress Administration helped create or improve parks, among other activities. One such project involved moving cemetery walls, crypts and grave markers to create this jetty. (You will also see headstones in Walk 18 – their use wasn't restricted to the Marina!)

6 Backtrack to Lyon Street. Cross Marina Boulevard. Explore the Exploratorium, if you'd like to.

At this science museum that seems like a fun house, explore mysteries of sight, sound, touch and perception. Dive into sonic soup or explore total darkness in the Tactile Dome, or lose your perspective in an optical illusion.
EXPLORATORIUM;
www.exploratorium.edu

7 When you've finished, continue on through the apparent ruins and lagoon, which is really the Palace of Fine Arts, 3601 Lyon Street.

These "ruins" were designed to look old from the day they were born. Architect Bernard Maybeck (1862-1957) used his creation to anchor the western end of the Panama-Pacific International Exposition with the towering presence of ancient Italy. Built in plaster and stucco rather than granite or marble, the ruins need regular renovation, but they are all that's left of the once vast fairgrounds.

8 From Bay Street (the southern edge of the Palace of Fine Arts), walk east to Divisadero Street and turn right on Divisadero. Turn left on Chestnut Street, where the beautiful people stop for coffee or dinner or a movie, and where you can catch the No. 30 Muni bus.

OPPOSITE: THE APPARENT RUINS OF THE PALACE OF FINE ARTS

WALK 22

The Presidio – from Cannons to Light Sabres

After more than 200 years as a military base, the Presidio has made the transition to an eco-friendly arty future – with a somewhat haunted past.

For centuries, the Spanish believed they had rights to possess the Americas and convert them to Christianity, but their resources were stretched thin. With plenty of gold and silver, and Indians organized to work in Mexico and Peru, they saw little benefit in venturing north to what is now California. In the 1770s, in a last ditch (and ultimately unsuccessful) attempt to shore up the empire against incursions from Russian whalers, French fur traders and English explorers, they sent a few Franciscan missionaries and a few soldiers to establish colonies and fortifications here. The Mission (see Walk 16) and the Presidio are the two oldest settlements in San Francisco. From 1776 to 1994, the Presidio was a military base that guarded the entrance to the bay, first for the Spanish, then the Mexicans, and finally the US. Since decommissioning in 1994, it's become an urban refuge for environmental and non-profit organizations, a lucky find in the residential rental market, the home of *Star Wars* creator George Lucas's Letterman Digital Arts Center, and a great park. It's also home to a ghost or two (or more).

Take the No. 29 Muni bus to the Officers' Club and Visitor Center, Moraga Avenue. Or take the more frequent No. 41 to its terminus at Lyon and Greenwich, walk to the Lombard Gate, then take the PresidiGo shuttle. Note: this walk takes in only a bit of the Presidio's 1,491 acres (605 hectares); to see more, catch the free PresidiGo shuttle bus (www.presidio.gov/directions/presidigo.htm).

The posters in the Visitor Center give an excellent overview of the Presidio and its history. The signs, however, do not mention the ghost of María de la Concepción Marcela Argüello. Can you see her gliding across the dance floor? Expert ghost busters can. Who was Concepción? Cheerful and vivacious, she was the 15-year-old daughter of the Spanish *comandante* when, in spring 1806, Russian aristocrat Nikolai Petrovich Rezanov sailed into San Francisco Bay, in search of food for his starving compatriots in Sitka, Alaska. By the time he left six weeks later, Nikolai and Concepción were in love. The smitten couple received linguistic assistance from the Russian's German physician who could talk to Concepción's Spanish priest in Latin. Religious differences were not so easy to resolve. For the couple to marry, Rezanov needed dispensation from the Pope and the Russian emperor. With this resolve, he sailed away, and Concepción waited patiently for his return. Time passed, but she never looked at other suitors. We do not know if she was ever told that Rezanov had died en route to St Petersburg. We do know that she became a Dominican nun, and remained in the sisterhood until her death 50 years later. Now she dances when the dance floor is empty.

WHERE TO EAT

1 BOWLING ALLEY,
Montgomery Street, Main Post Parade Ground;
Tel: 1-415-561-2695.
Nothing fancy – the kind of food that goes with bowling. $

2 STARBUCKS,
Letterman Digital Arts Center;
Tel: 1-415-441-1740.
Standard Starbucks in a gorgeous setting, popular with those who work in the Center. $

3 TERRASSE CAFÉ
at Transit Center, off Lincoln Boulevard;
Tel: 1-415-922-3463.
More restaurant than cafe, with fancy and tasty meals. $$

2 Leaving the Officers' Club, the expanse in front of you is the main Parade Ground. Turn right on Moraga Avenue to Funston Avenue.

Pershing Hall, on the right, is named for General Pershing, who was on duty in Mexico when his house burned down and his family perished. The Presidio then established its own fire department.

OPPOSITE: CIVIL WAR ERA OFFICERS' HOUSES AT THE PRESIDIO

DISTANCE **2 miles (3.3km)**

ALLOW **2.5 hours**

START **Officers' Club and Visitor Center**

FINISH **Officers' Club and Visitor Center**

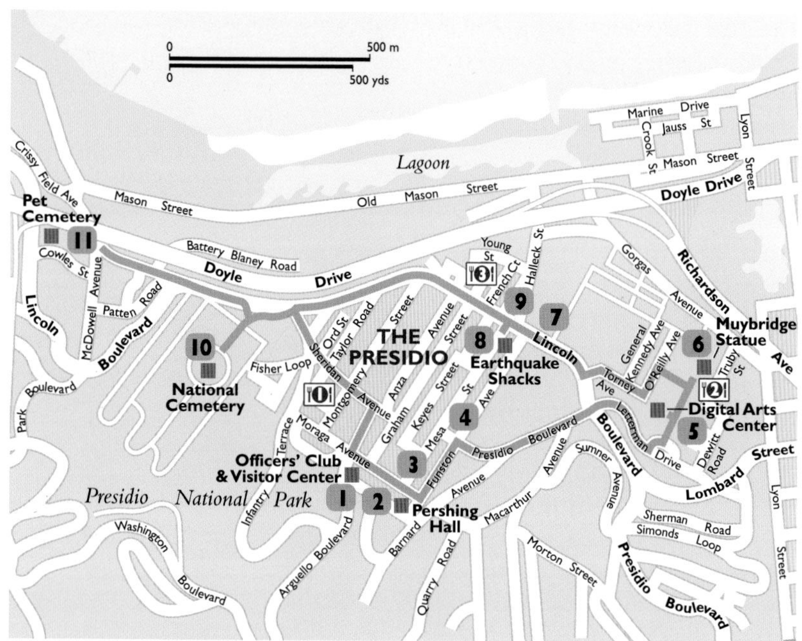

3 Turn left on Funston Avenue.

The avenue is named for Frederick Funston (1865-1917), who was the ranking army commander in San Francisco when disaster struck in 1906. By sending troops into the city to help police and fire fighters, Funston overstepped legal bounds for military action in civilian society – but he was highly praised for the quick response and successful action.

The trees across the street seem typical of the Presidio that you see today but, until the 1870s, few trees grew on the sand dunes here. After the Civil War (1861-65) nearly tore the nation apart, the government felt a need to demonstrate strength and confidence. Tree planting here was part of that demonstration. Likewise, the officers' houses along Funston (now offices for small organizations and consulting firms) had originally faced in towards the Parade Ground, but in the 1870s,

the "front" porches were moved to the back (as they are today), so that the army could look out on the city with a show of pride.

4 Turn right on Presidio Boulevard, then veer right on Letterman Drive. Veer left again to the Letterman Digital Arts Center.

In the courtyard to the left is Yoda, and in the lobby behind, you'll see Darth Vader, King Kong and other movie stars.

Step back and look at the buildings around you: they are new but were designed to blend in with the tones, textures and spirit of the old Presidio. Does it work? And speaking of spirits, this is another hotbed of ghosts. Ghosts have been seen milling about, waiting to enter the World War II era Letterman Hospital that was here before Yoda.

5 Continue down through the landscaped gardens and office buildings to the statue of Eadweard J Muybridge and the view out to the Palace of Fine Arts.

English photographer Muybridge (1830-1904) is commemorated here, in the midst of the Letterman Digital Arts Center, for his work in capturing motion. He used fast-frame photography to document whether all four of a horse's hooves leave the ground during a gallop. Behind the statue is the location of a major 1906 refugee camp.

6 Turn left on the path through the office buildings. At O'Reilly Avenue, turn left, then a quick right at Torney Avenue. The corner house was for the family of the ranking medical officer at the Army General Hospital; in 1906, this was Lt Col George H Torney. His heroic actions in helping the disaster-torn city escape major public health woes and epidemics won him wide admiration. Continue on Torney, then veer right to Lincoln Boulevard. Stop at the newly renewed creek bed.

As part of the plan to transform the former military base into an eco-friendly sustainable park, an old army waste dump was recently cleaned up, and this creek is out in the air again!

ABOVE: STATUE OF YODA ATOP THE FOUNTAIN AT THE LETTERMAN DIGITAL ARTS CENTER

7 Cross Lincoln Boulevard and continue to Mesa Street. Turn left (uphill) at Mesa.

The octagonal building on the left was the surgery attached to the Civil War-era hospital. Before electric lights, an octagon was considered ideal for letting in as much sunlight as possible.

Just around from the octagon are two little green "Earthquake shacks". After the earthquake of 18 April 1906 the city burned for days and 200,000 or more were left homeless. Water mains and sewer pipes were broken. Food supplies were sporadic. Indoor fires were banned until chimneys were checked. Thousands left town until services were restored. For some, the only option was to camp in a park. Relief officials worried that refugees would get accustomed to an easy life of free food (weak coffee, cold meat and sand blowing into your beans, not to mention the queues) and free shelter (tents sitting in mud, shared latrines). By September, most refugees had found their own shelter, but for those still in need, it was time to build something more substantial. Five thousand of these shacks were manufactured, to house a few more than 17,000 refugees.

8 Backtrack to Lincoln Boulevard, and walk past the Fire Station, on the right at Keyes Avenue, across from the Transit Center.

Where the First Republic Bank branch is now located used to be a stockade – ghosts of both prisoners and guards have been spotted in the vicinity. Also, on at least one occasion, a bus driver picked up a military officer who flagged him down here. When he looked in the rear-view mirror, the passenger had vanished.

9 Continue on Lincoln to the San Francisco National Cemetery.

Other than at Mission Dolores, this is the only cemetery still within San Francisco. Soldiers have been buried here since 1849. There are now 30,000 graves. When the ghost-busters (they call themselves intuitive archaeologists) studied the Presidio, they didn't come here, but it's best not to be found here after dark. (The gates close at 16.30.)

10 It's a long walk, but to detour to the Pet Cemetery, turn left on Lincoln as you exit the cemetery. Veer slightly right on Crissy Field Avenue to the bottom of the hill. (Or, follow the signs for the Stables. From the stables, go downhill on McDowell Avenue.)

This is the final resting place of Presidio humans' beloved pets, including Big Red Dog, Ole Brown Dog, Champagne, Samoyeds Princess Kiska and Stoli, and Boris the tortoise, among others.

11 Backtrack to the National Cemetery. Leaving the National Cemetery, to return to the starting point, veer right on Sheridan Avenue. At the main Parade Ground, turn right to get back to the Officers' Club or turn left to the Transit Center.

OPPOSITE: SAN FRANCISCO NATIONAL CEMETERY, WHERE SOLDIERS HAVE BEEN BURIED SINCE 1849

WALK
23

Against All Odds – the Golden Gate Bridge

To those who said, "It can't be done!" and "We don't want it!", visionary bridge-builder Joseph Strauss replied: "Don't be afraid to dream!"

It almost didn't get built, but now we love, hate, fear, use and celebrate the Golden Gate Bridge. On the day before it opened to vehicles, the city threw a party and 200,000 people attended. From 6am to 6pm on 27 May 1937, everyone came to try out the bridge in their own special way. There were babies in prams, twins on roller skates, boy scouts, dancers, people walking backwards, people walking arm-in-arm, and a pet flea carried across in its own plastic bag. Florentine Calegeri walked both ways on stilts. Milton Pilhashay tried to push a pillbox across with his nose but gave up after about 100ft (30m). Walter Farlin was the first to sprint the distance from the San Francisco toll gates to Marin and back, in 17 minutes. History did not record the first to sneak across without paying the toll. The price was five cents each way and the coin boxes filled so fast they had to be replaced with buckets. It's free to walk across today. But whether you've got a pet flea or a baby in a pram, be sure to wear plenty of warm layers – it can be cold and windy!

Take the No. 28 or 29 Muni bus or any Golden Gate Transit bus, then walk to the Information Center Plaza. Check out the cross section of cable and the statue of world-renowned bridge-builder Joseph Strauss (1870-1938).

Emperor Joshua Norton (1819-80) was pronounced insane for (among other things) his 1872 proclamation that a bridge should be built to Sausalito (see Walk 1). Fifty years later, the battle to build the bridge had begun, and Joseph Strauss was leading the charge.

Strauss was a small man – barely 5ft (1.5m) tall – with big dreams. When city engineer Michael O'Shaughnessy first approached Strauss, O'Shaughnessy said: "Everybody says it can't be done and that it would cost over $100,000,000 if it could be done." O'Shaughnessy expected a flat refusal. Instead, Strauss was hooked.

Strauss's associates were better designers and engineers than he. His real contribution was his relentless push to convince the many naysayers. "This is a bridge that no one needs," they said. The population north of San Francisco was sparse, and the ferry service across the bay was excellent. Car dealers hoped to increase sales, so they supported it, as did real estate speculators. But loggers and environmentalists didn't want the increased traffic the bridge would bring.

"It will be physically impossible," they said. No suspension bridge this long had ever been built, nor had a bridge been built over open ocean. It would need to withstand high winds and earthquakes. The flow of water through the narrows amounts to 528 billion gallons (2 billion m^3) every six hours, with only a 20-60 minute calm between tides – resulting in currents that typically exceed 5.6mph (9km/h).

The north tower wouldn't be difficult to build – it would sit on dry land. But the south tower would need to sit one-quarter mile (0.4km) offshore, under 65ft (20m) of turbulent water. One geologist, from the University of California at Berkeley, determined that the bedrock would support the towers; another, from Stanford University, insisted the bedrock was like pudding. Thirteen engineers – including Michael O'Shaughnessy – submitted statements that the bridge could not be built.

"It will be too expensive," they said. O'Shaughnessy had said it would cost a hundred million dollars; Strauss said it could be done for thirty-five (and because it was built during the Depression, when wages and prices

OPPOSITE: THE GOLDEN GATE BRIDGE SPANS OPEN OCEAN; ABOVE: BRIDGE-BUILDER JOSEPH STRAUSS

DISTANCE **2 miles (3.2km) – a hill and stairs**

ALLOW **2 hours, an extra hour if you walk all the way across the bridge**

START **Golden Gate Bridge Information Center Plaza**

FINISH **Golden Gate Bridge Information Center Plaza**

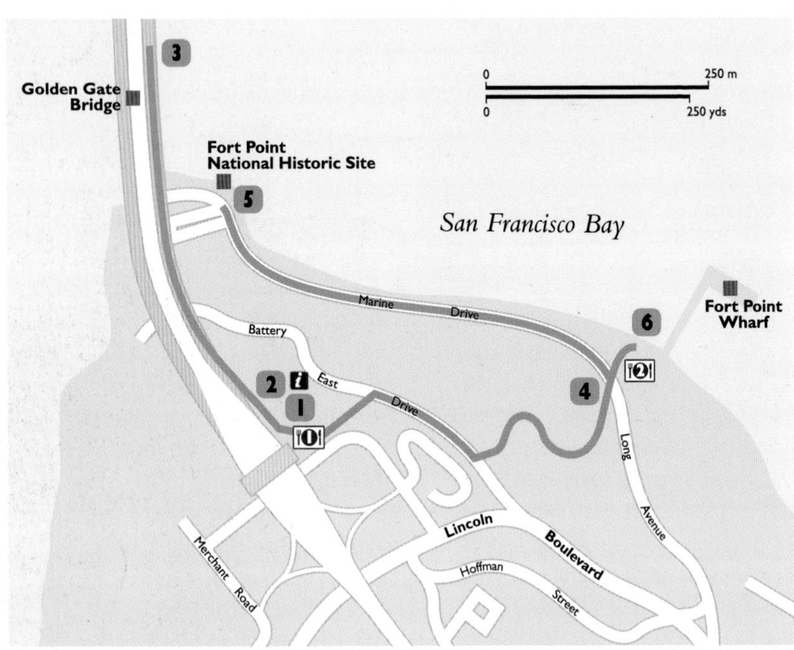

were low, it came in under budget). It received no government funding. Even after voters agreed to float bonds to finance construction, no one wanted to buy the bonds! (Strauss convinced A P Giannini of the Bank of America to buy a substantial portion; see Walk 1.)

Once the plans were approved and the bonds sold, now it had to be built. Only San Franciscans were hired for all but the most skilled jobs. Slackers were fired. Construction totalled an estimated twenty-five million man hours.

Strauss made safety a top priority. This was among the first major building projects where hard hats were required. $80,000 was spent on hanging a safety net and – every time but one – the safety net did its job, catching 19 men (making them members of the "Halfway-to-Hell Club"). But 11 men did die (a very low number by industry standards): one man was crushed by machinery; ten more were killed when the platform they were working on ripped through the safety net.

OPPOSITE: EMBLEMATIC OF SAN FRANCISCO, THE GOLDEN GATE BRIDGE IS A FEAT OF ENGINEERING

WHERE TO EAT

1 BRIDGE CAFÉ,
At the Information Center;
No phone.
Not the friendliest service but the sandwiches are good. Grab a light snack to takeaway. $

2 WARMING HUT,
Along the water's edge;
Tel: 1-415-561-3040.
Light fare in a comfortable atmosphere. On cool days, sit inside but if there's sunshine, try to grab a spot outside. $

2 Venture out on the bridge – cross all the way, or not, as you please.

The bridge's statistics are staggering. Its main span is 4,200ft (1,280m) – the longest single span until 1964. The length of the entire suspended structure is 6,450ft (1,966m), and all of this hangs (literally) on 80,000 miles (129,000km) of cable wire – enough to wrap around the earth several times.

As it was designed to do, the Golden Gate Bridge flexes with heavy traffic, expands and contracts as temperatures rise and fall, and sways from side to side in the wind. It has closed on only three occasions due to weather, in each case when winds reached 69-75 mph (110-120km/h): on 1 December 1951 (closed for three hours); on 23 December 1982 (closed for almost two hours); and on 3 December 1983 (closed for 3 hours and 27 minutes). The bridge suffered no structural damage on these occasions, although officials were concerned that gusting winds would result in traffic accidents.

The Art Deco towers, rising 746ft (227m) above the water, were designed using steel plates covering the framing that get smaller as they go up, creating an illusion of even greater height than in reality. The towers are hollow, with elevators for maintenance crews inside, and each includes some 600,000 rivets.

Who chose this colour? The military wanted yellow and black stripes, others argued for metallic silver (standard bridge colour). Strauss wanted gold to match the name. It was architect Irving Morrow who chose international orange because it enhanced the tones of the Marin Headlands, and could be easily seen through dense fogs.

Another statistic – now restricted information to discourage copy-cats – is the number of individuals who have jumped. It's said that in 1973, after the 499th confirmed death, the police put up a round-the-clock death watch, and some 14 potential jumpers vied (unsuccessfully) for the coveted place of number 500 – one even wore the number 500 pinned to his shirt.

Now, help boxes are posted along the way, video monitors scan constantly, police cars sweep back and forth across the bridge, and plain clothes officers traverse by bike, all on the look out for worrisome activities. Bridge officials are working on plans to install jump barriers – much to the annoyance of many.

3 Backtrack to the Information Plaza, then follow the signs to Fort Point.

Notice the earthwork batteries along the path, part of a late-19th-century system of guns trained on the entrance to the bay. If you look up, you might also notice a hawk soaring on the wind currents.

4 From the bottom of the stairs, turn left towards Fort Point.

Why was a fort built under the bridge? In fact, the fort was there first. Built between 1853 and 1861, Fort Point has perched at the edge of the entry to the bay, and waited for an enemy that has never come. Original bridge plans called for tearing down Fort Point but Strauss insisted on creating a special arch over the point so that the two could coexist.

www.nps.gov/fopo/historyculture

If the crashing of the waves at the point beyond the fort seems familiar, remember the movie *Vertigo*. Madeleine, tormented with dreams of Carlotta, tries to drown herself in the waters off the point. Scottie rescues her.

5 Backtrack along Marine Drive to the Fort Point Wharf (1908).

If you would like to keep walking, continue along the coastal pathway. This is the restored habitat area of Crissy Field (formerly a military airfield), and especially beautiful in springtime. Backtrack the way you came.

6 Return uphill following the signs to the Information Plaza, where you can catch the No. 28 or 29 Muni bus or any Golden Gate Transit bus back into town.

ABOVE: FORT POINT WAS BUILT TO PROTECT THE HARBOUR DURING AND AFTER THE AMERICAN CIVIL WAR

WALK 24

Sundown at Land's End

A spectacular walk in an awesome setting that explores the point where San Francisco juts into the "Sundown Sea" .

Enjoy one outstanding view after another of what Native Americans called the "Sundown Sea". Walk along a little forested path that feels like your own secret hideaway. Visit a museum modelled on the 18th-century Palais de la Légion d'Honneur in Paris, but this one is right in the middle of a golf course. Stroll through the ruins of rich eccentric Adolph Sutro's cliff-top estate. Walk along the route of his defunct train route, built to bring the masses from downtown to enjoy an enormous saltwater swimming pool (now in ruins). Hear the crash of waves and the bleat of fog horns. Go inside a dark hut to see brilliant real-time images of beach, surf and seagulls, projected using a technique developed by Leonardo da Vinci. Note that the Legion of Honor here and the de Young in Golden Gate Park (see Walk 19) are sister museums: admission tickets to the Legion may be used on the same day for entrance to the de Young. Also, show your transit pass or transfer to receive a discount. If you can, try to do this walk at low tide to see the shipwrecks, and at midday to avoid the fog.

1 **Take the No. 1 bus to the terminus at Geary Street and 32nd Avenue. Backtrack on 32nd one block to Clement Street, turn left (at the edge of the golf course) to 34th Avenue, turn right on Legion of Honor Drive, and walk through the golf course to the Legion of Honor Museum.**

Starving art student turned social grande dame and benefactor Alma de Bretteville Spreckels fell in love with the French Pavilion at the 1915 Panama-Pacific International Exposition. As she was married to sugar magnate Adolph B Spreckels (1857-1924), she could afford to do something about it. With permission from France, she had a replica built here. Believing it her mission to make art accessible to the public, she not only underwrote the construction, but then donated much of her own collection, including *The Thinker* (in the front courtyard) and other Rodin sculptures. (See the Spreckels residence in Walk 15.)

Lovers of Alfred Hitchcock's *Vertigo* might look for the painting of Carlotta Valdez that so fascinated Madeleine – but it's not here, and never was.

LEGION OF HONOR MUSEUM; www.famsf.org/legion

2 **Cross the car park in front of the museum to see the downtown views, then circle back to the right along the sidewalk to the Holocaust Memorial.**

Take the short road down at the left of the Memorial and then turn left on

El Camino del Mar (which looks like a car park here) and continue through to the end, where it becomes a forested footpath. Shortly, follow the signs to turn right to the Coast Trail. Turn left on the Coast Trail, following signs to Sutro Baths and the *USS San Francisco*.

This is actually the Lincoln Highway, the nation's first transcontinental highway, which ended here in Lincoln Park. The Coast Trail follows the railbed of the "Sutro Railroad". Until the Sutro trolley line was built, this area was accessible only to those who could afford to rent or own a horse or carriage, and spend an entire day here.

Looking at the ocean, it won't surprise you that pounding surf, frequent fog and submerged rock outcroppings combine for danger. At low tide, you may catch a

OPPOSITE: THE RUINS OF SUTRO BATHS; ABOVE: RODIN'S *THE THINKER* AT THE LEGION OF HONOR MUSEUM

DISTANCE 3 miles (5km) – some hills and stairs

ALLOW Half a day, plus 2 hours if you visit the Legion of Honor Museum

START Geary Street and 32nd Avenue

FINISH Fulton Street

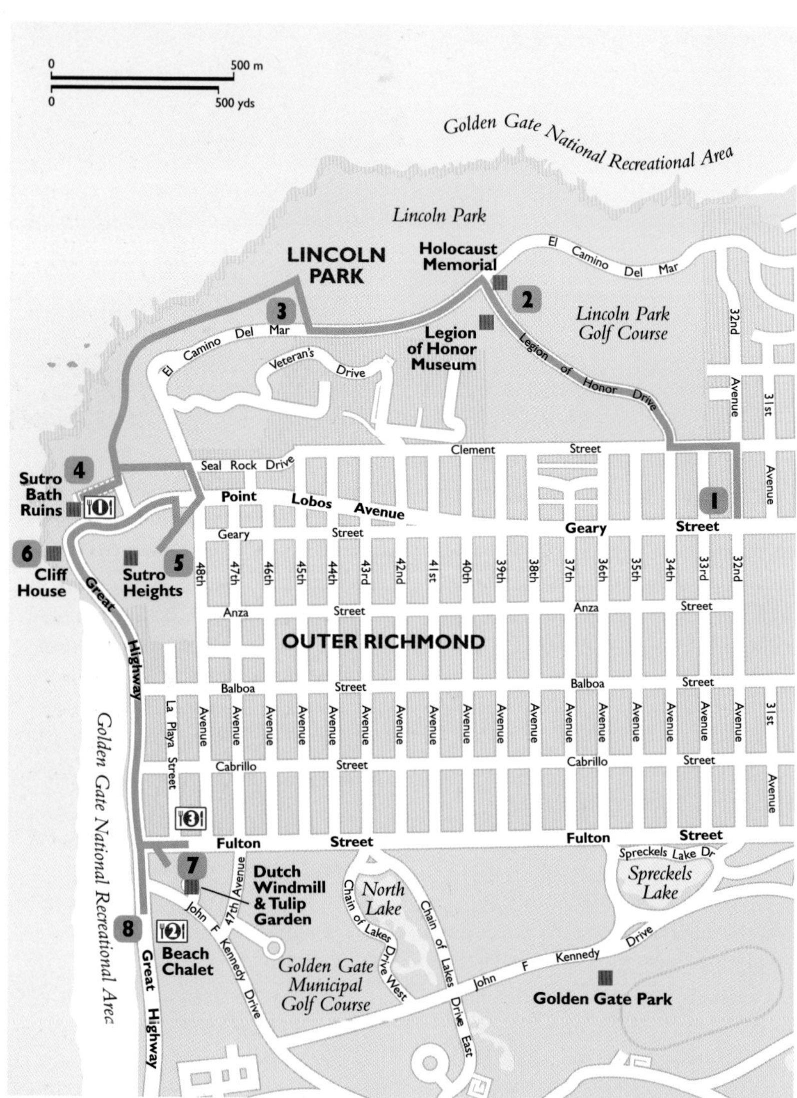

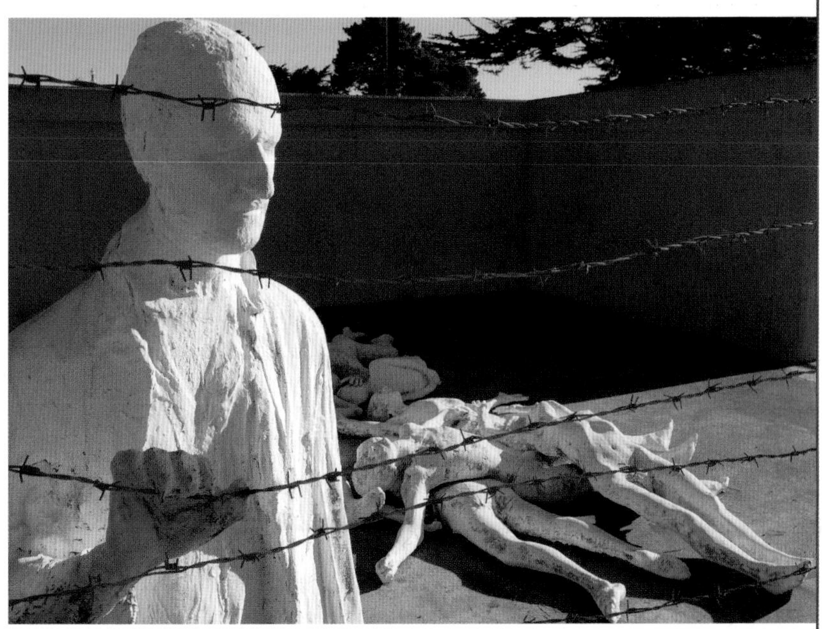

glimpse of shipwrecks. In 1901, the *City of Rio de Janeiro* crashed near Mile Rock (just offshore to the north-west of Lands End), and soon after, a lighthouse was built, not without difficulty. Mile Rock also has a foghorn that gives a two-second blast of "C" every 30 seconds. (Other foghorns blast from both the midspan and the south tower of the Golden Gate Bridge, and from north-west and south-east points of Alcatraz.)

3 Continue on the Coast Trail, then turn right following signs to the Ruins of Sutro Baths.

The ruins you see now are all that is left of what was once an amazing and complete entertainment centre (1896-1966). A glass roof protected broad promenades, staircases, a natural history museum, flowers and palms, an amphitheatre, Egyptian mummies (both wrapped and unwrapped), stuffed birds and coin collections from the elements. The building could hold 25,000 visitors. More than 500 private dressing rooms with soap, towels, showers, lockers and woollen bathing suits were available for up to 1,600 bathers. They could enjoy six saltwater tanks and a freshwater plunge. It cost $0.25 to swim, or $0.10 to watch. As the novelty wore off and attendance dropped, the cost of maintenance became greater than the income generated. For a while, the baths were converted into a skating rink. Eventually, in 1966, as the baths were being demolished, a fire (possibly arson) took it all down. The elements continue to erode what is left.

ABOVE: THE HOLOCAUST MEMORIAL IN LINCOLN PARK

WHERE TO EAT

LOUIS',
902 Point Lobos Avenue;
Tel: 1-415-387-6330.
Cash only (no credit cards!) at this popular place for breakfast or lunch. $

BEACH CHALET,
1000 Great Highway;
Tel: 1-415-386-8439.
Cafe or brew pub and restaurant: two options but both get crowded on sunny days. $$

SAFEWAY,
850 La Playa Street at Fulton;
Tel: 1-415-387-4664.
Pick up salads, sandwiches and picnic food at the deli here. $

4 Backtrack uphill from the baths and to the traffic signal at the corner of Point Lobos Avenue and 48th Avenue. Cross Point Lobos, and turn into the lion-guarded gate to Sutro Heights.

This was once the home of Adolph Sutro (1830-98), German immigrant, mining engineer, bibliophile, arborist and mayor. His heirs were land-rich but cash-poor, so they sold it to the city, who promptly tore down the hard-to-maintain house and garden statuary.

Sutro made his fortune by designing a tunnel that could drain and ventilate underground silver mines in Nevada. When he returned to San Francisco in the 1860s, his millions didn't buy him acceptance with the Nob Hill snobs. His response? Clean up politics (he served one less-than-successful term as mayor – the political machinery didn't know what to do with "clean"). He also improved the city by planting thousands of trees, and made exercise and outside activities available to all. He opened the grounds of his home to the public (to avoid litter, guests were required to leave their picnic baskets at the gate). He built the trolley line, he built the Baths, and he bought the Cliff House (see below).

5 After exploring Sutro Heights, exit and cross to the other side of Point Lobos Avenue again, and proceed downhill along the pavement to the Cliff House.

The rather bland exterior of this, the most recent of several Cliff Houses on the site, belies the magnificent views from inside. Earlier Cliff Houses fell victim to wind and saltwater, chimney fires, construction fires and, on one occasion, the unparalleled shipwreck on the rocks below of the ocean-going schooner *Parallel*, that happened to be loaded with kerosene, a cask of dynamite caps, and 1,685 50lb (23kg) casks of gunpowder, with a combined weight of about 42 tons (38 metric tons).

Tucked behind the Cliff House is the camera obscura. Based on a design by Leonardo da Vinci, a series of rotating mirrors and lenses project a crisp view of the world outside on a huge parabolic dish. Amazing views of surf and surfers, seagulls and passersby.

6 **Continue downhill via the Great Highway or Ocean Beach. (It's not a good beach for swimming – there are riptides, an undertow and rogue waves, not to mention the cold!) At Fulton Street, cross the Great Highway and enter Golden Gate Park to visit the Dutch Windmill and Tulip Garden.**

The windmill was built (in 1901) so the city wouldn't have to buy water to irrigate the park at exorbitant rates from the Spring Valley Water Company, which had a monopoly. At 75ft (23m) in height, it has long been a recognizable landmark for ships approaching the Golden Gate. It was successful almost immediately, and a second windmill was built just to the south in 1905 (the "Murphy" windmill, named for the wealthy San Francisco banker who funded it). By 1913, electric pumps obviated the need for the windmills, and they fell into disuse and disrepair. One storm in the 1930s blew the vanes off.

7 **Backtrack to the Great Highway, turn left along to the Beach Chalet, 1000 Great Highway.**

Designed by Willis Polk (see Walk 15), this opened in 1925 to provide changing rooms for beach-goers. In 1936, Lucien Labaudt created the frescoes and mosaics.

8 **Backtrack to Fulton Street and turn right to catch the No. 5 Fulton bus back downtown.**

ABOVE: BEACH CHALET FRESCO, DESIGNED BY LUCIEN LABAUDT IN 1936

CLIFF HOUSE MAKES UP FOR ITS BLAND EXTERIOR WITH COMMANDING VIEWS OF THE PACIFIC COAST

INDEX

ACKNOWLEDGEMENTS

The Automobile Association wishes to thank the following photographers and organisations for their assistance in the preparation of this book.
Abbreviations for the picture credits are as follows – (AA) AA World Travel Library
Front Cover: Curtis Martin/Lonely Planet Images; 3 Stephen Saks Photography/Alamy; 7 Curtis Martin/Lonely Planet Images; 8 Sergio Lanza/Fotolibra; 11 Julian Page/Fotolibra; 13 Sergio Lanza/Fotolibra; 14 Sergio Lanza/Fotolibra; 18 Eileen Keremitsis; 20/21 SIME/Frances Stephane/4Corners Images; 22 Rick Gerharter/Lonely Planet Images; 23 Eileen Keremitsis; 25 Eileen Keremitsis; 27 Anthony Pidgeon/Lonely Planet Images; 28 Paul Collis/Alamy; 31 Eileen Keremitsis; 33 Julian Page/Fotolibra; 34/35 Julian Page/Fotolibra; 36 Julian Page/Fotolibra; 37 Eileen Keremitsis; 41 Julian Page/Fotolibra; 42 World Pictures/Photoshot; 45 John Lander/Alamy; 46 Anthony Pidgeon/Lonely Planet Images; 48/49 Roberto Soncin Gerometta/Alamy; 50 Ray Laskowitz/Lonely Planet Images; 53 Anthony Pidgeon/Lonely Planet Images; 55 World Pictures/Photoshot; 56 David R Frazier Photolibrary, Inc/Alamy; 57 Eileen Keremitsis; 59 John Elk III/Lonely Planet Images; 60 World Pictures/Photoshot; 62/63 Holger Leue/Lonely Planet Images; 64 David R Frazier Photolibrary, Inc./Alamy; 67 Richard I'Anson/Lonely Planet Images; 69 Eileen Keremitsis; 70 Fabian Gonzales Editorial/Alamy; 71 Anthony Pidgeon/Lonely Planet Images; 73 Sergio Lanza/Fotolibra; 75 Clive Sawyer; 76/77 Sergio Lanza/Fotolibra; 78 Art Kowalsky/Alamy; 81 Eileen Keremitsis; 82 Clive Sawyer; 84 Rick Gerharter/Lonely Planet Images; 85 Renaud Visage / Alamy; 87 Lee Beel/Fotolibra; 88 Richard Cummins/Lonely Planet Images; 90/91 Rick Gerharter/Lonely Planet Images; 92 SIME/Giovanni Simeone/4Corners Images; 93 Richard Cummins/Lonely Planet Images; 96 Eileen Keremitsis; 97 Eileen Keremitsis; 98 Sergio Lanza/Fotolibra; 99 Sergio Lanza/Fotolibra; 101 Sergio Lanza/Fotolibra; 104/105 Ei Katsumata/Alamy; 106 Ron Scherl/Fotolibra; 109 Ron Scherl/Fotolibra; 110 Eileen Keremitsis; 112 Anthony Pidgeon/Lonely Planet Images; 113 Eileen Keremitsis; 116 John Lander/Alamy; 118/119 Clive Sawyer; 120 Curtis Martin/Lonely Planet Images; 123 Eileen Keremitsis; 125 Sergio Lanza/Fotolibra; 126 Eileen Keremitsis; 127 Sergio Lanza/Fotolibra; 130/131 Gary Crabbe/Alamy; 132/133 Garry Gay/Alamy; 134 Mike Savage/Fotolibra; 135 Ron Scherl/Fotolibra; 137 Ron Scherl/Fotolibra; 139 Richard Cummins/Lonely Planet Images; 140 Eileen Keremitsis; 143 Richard Cummins/Lonely Planet Images; 144 Richard Wong/www.rwongphoto.com/Alamy; 145 Clive Sawyer; 146/147 Danita Delimont/Alamy; 148 Chuck Nacke/Alamy; 149 Eileen Keremitsis; 153 Ionas Kaltenbach/Lonely Planet Images; 154 Eileen Keremitsis; 157 Eileen Keremitsis; 159 Gary Crabbe/Alamy; 160 World Pictures/Photoshot; 161 Eileen Keremitsis; 163 Paul Harris/Getty Images; 165 4Corners/Borchi Massimo; 166 Anthony Pidgeon/Lonely Planet Images; 167 Amritaphotos/Alamy; 169 ABN Stock Image /Alamy; 171 Eileen Keremitsis; 172/173 Danita Delimont/Alamy.
Every effort has been made to trace the copyright holders, and we apologize in advance for any unintentional omissions or errors. We would be pleased to apply any corrections in any following edition of this publication.